a stutterer's story

Frederick Pemberton Murray, Ph.D.
Retired from
Communication Disorders Department
University of New Hampshire

with Susan Goodwillie Edwards

Stuttering Foundation of America

A STUTTERER'S STORY

First Printing — 1980
Second Printing — 1991
Third Printing — 1994

Published by

Stuttering Foundation of America
P.O. Box 11749
Memphis, Tennessee 38111

Library of Congress Catalog Card No. 80-80688
ISBN 0-933388-30-6

The Stuttering Foundation of America is a non-profit
charitable organization dedicated to the prevention and
treatment of stuttering.

*To **all who stutter***

The author in 1989.

Preface

Stuttering, that ancient anomaly of speech that has afflicted and twisted the lives of countless persons down through the ages, remains a problem, which, to date, can only be partially explained. This remains true despite the current assertions of just-upon-the-scene enthusiasts who claim miraculous results via so-called "new" methods of therapy. Fluency of speech, so easy to achieve under carefully contrived conditions, often collapses like a house of cards when the stutterer interacts in daily life situations involving communicative pressure.

This is the story of a severe stutterer, now adequately fluent, who, having attained fragile fluency several times, tried to assemble the pieces of wreckage following each relapse and to construct something substantial and lasting from them. This called for searching and self-inquiry. Some of these quests led toward better organized and more helpful types of therapy. Others led inward in a scrutinization for more self-knowledge.

The message herein is one of hope and encouragement, provided that the stutterer is ready to give up his entrenched illusion of the nonexistent "perfect cure" and to begin to assemble, within himself, that which is needed in order to manage effectively what heretofore has overwhelmed him. Such sincere efforts will, of themselves, kindle and maintain the flame of human spirit, for without it, nothing worthwhile can be accomplished.

Contents

The author in 1942.

1

Its Beginning

Unlike most stuttering, mine began violently. The transition from completely normal to completely abnormal speech occurred overnight while I was sleeping. Whenever I now hear the expression, "different as night and day," I think wryly of what that June night in 1928 and the following morning have meant to me.

We had just returned to my family's summer home in Marin County, California, from a visit to Yosemite National Park. I was little more than two and a half years old, so I had not been able to do as much walking and climbing in that beautiful wilderness as my brother, who was twelve; but, even at that age, I loved traveling, and this trip had been a happy one for me. Only one thing had gone wrong. The day before we were to leave Yosemite I had had an unusually severe nosebleed, which may have been related to the high altitude. However, the next day, although my mother said I was rather pale, I seemed fine, and after lunch the four of us started our long trip home.

Marin is a county just north of San Francisco. To get there we had to drive two hundred miles, and then, being in the pre-bridge days, take a ferry across San Francisco Bay. That evening as we approached the ferry landing on the Richmond side of the bay we saw that our boat, the last run of the day, was already pulling away from the dock. This must have upset my parents, because it meant we had to drive around the bay to another landing from which we would have to take two ferries to reach the Marin County shore. Even though it was late and I should have been tired, my parents said I was delighted to have two boat rides instead of one. Finally we were home, and my mother tucked me into bed.

When she woke me the next morning, she was horrified to discover that I could not say a single word. Out of my mouth came nothing but meaningless, stroke-like gurgles. I, too, must have been badly frightened. My parents called a doctor from the nearby town of San Rafael who came as quickly as he could. After examining me, he said, "There's been some kind of terrific upheaval in this boy's nervous system. I want him kept relaxed and quiet in bed for several days. And keep other people away from him."

After three or four days, my parents heard a few stuttered words in the midst of my incomprehensible jabbering and frequent spasms. Gradually, the nonsensical sounds began to disappear. I spoke in words, phrases, and short sentences again, but there were frequent breaks, or blocks, in the sentences. I had become a stutterer.

■ ────────────────────────────────────── ■

If, as a speech pathologist, I were shown a case like this one today, I would hope that the summoned physician might follow the advice of my late colleague, Dr. Charles Bluemel, and immediately put the child under heavy sedation that would keep him relatively unconscious for a week or ten days, feeding him intravenously, on the chance that his nervous system could be relaxed and rested and that his symptoms would disappear.

I will go into detail about this in Chapters 20 and 23, but for the moment it is enough to say that, while there continues to be disagreement in the speech field about the cause of stuttering, I believe that it has an organic basis. I think it, in its simplest form, is the result of a weakness in the nervous system which often begins to manifest itself about the time a child begins to speak in complete sentences, at age three or four. In most instances the disorder begins gradually, with slight and occasional repetitions or prolongations of words or syllables.

While my early speech was apparently normal, there are factors that indicate I may have had an imperfectly operating nervous system. When my mother was young, she had been told by her doctor that her nervous system seemed overreactive and that the problem could be hereditary. As a baby I had a number of digestive troubles. When I learned to walk I often walked on my toes, a phenomenon associated with a malfunctioning nervous system. There were also signs of my being hypertensive.

In the years since 1928, as my knowledge and experience in the speech field developed, I have gone over the few facts that I have about my stuttering's abrupt beginning, trying to understand what happened to me. I believe that it was probably a weak nervous system's response to the Yosemite nosebleed, aggravated by the strain of the long trip home, and that something in my already vulnerable system may have snapped because of a blood deficiency in the brain. If I had been put under heavy sedation the following morning, I might have waked a week later, completely fluent, never to stutter again. Or, if the stuttering had been stopped on this occasion, it might have surfaced under another stress a year or two later. I will never know.

■ ────────────────────────────────────── ■

While my family situation was very comfortable materially, there were elements in our home that made life distressing for a small stutterer. My parents believed in the importance of social forms and traditions—the dancing classes, the tennis lessons, the debutante balls—all the complicated rites of the social set, filled with specific speech and behavior requirements that are easy for the assured and healthy, but nightmarish for the shy or disabled.

My parents were older than most of my friends' parents and less flexible in their ideas. I think they had not planned to have another child so long after the birth of my brother, who was ten when I was born, and had been very pleased with my arrival; I never felt that they didn't want me—it was my stuttering that they wished away.

Its extreme visibility was always embarrassing for them; if I had had a different problem, something that could have been hidden, things would have been easier. My stuttering interfered continually with my being able to move smoothly into the expected classes and parties where young San Francisco socialites received their training. These activities seemed so essential to my parents that they could not imagine my growing up successfully without them. Often they urged my participation, and then were frustrated when I failed. At the same time, they loved me, and, in the periods when social pressure was absent, I knew they understood that the handicap was not my fault.

My mother was a proud person, concerned with the welfare of her family and of her friends. In addition, she was constantly worrying, sensitive to most criticism, and resentful of any interference from strangers in our family's affairs. Fate thrust upon her shoulders many complex responsibilities. Looking back, I have come to realize that she did an amazing job in tackling a difficult situation. Many women would have fled from it. She supported and encouraged me in many ways, some of which I came to appreciate in later years. I owe her much gratitude.

Once, on a boat trip, a woman who had heard me stuttering asked my mother what had been done to help me. Many years later, my mother told me that she had wanted to leap overboard from shame. At the time she said nothing, but I was aware of her emotion. That experience, as well as similar experiences, soon established in me the first insidious feelings of guilt that pursue most stutterers and that are so difficult to banish in therapy—guilt for causing others pain.

My parents' marriage was, in my opinion, one of divergent personalities. The household tensions that arose from this were intensified by my brother's having a mind of his own. My father was generally an easy-going man with whom I usually got along well, but he could erupt violently when provoked. When I was small, the clashes that occurred periodically between members of my family frightened me. I was always concerned that trouble might begin. Once, when a boiling point had been reached and a physical struggle with a visiting relative seemed inevitable, I ran upstairs and hid under the bed of a friendly maid.

In San Francisco we lived in a gray stucco house, built in 1897, which sat on the hillside a mile from San Francisco Bay. From my bedroom window in the northeast corner I could look out and see Alcatraz Island with its lighthouse that flashed on and off all night long, the ferryboats plying back and forth on the bay, and, beyond the ferryboats, the hills of Berkeley. I loved that view.

The house was large, with seventeen rooms. My parents had been married there in 1914. It was a formal house, in contrast to the house in Marin County where we spent our summers. The country house had gardens and a sixty-foot swimming pool in which I learned to swim, an activity that has given me pleasure ever since.

The early relationship between my brother and me was largely determined by the ten-year difference in our ages and by differences in our health and temperaments. His robust health matched his vigorous spirit. I was a fearful, nervous boy who was often ill. My babyhood digestive troubles continued into childhood, and I had all sorts of other illnesses, including a double hernia at birth and ear infections so severe that once my eardrums had to be pierced—without anesthetic. (That made me afraid for years afterward of men who carried black bags.) When I was five, my appendix had to be taken out. The feeling then, and again three years later during a tonsillectomy, of being smothered under ether was so terrifying that I remember it today.

Like most older brothers, mine teased me at times. After a serious summer fire in the woods, he used to scare me by pretending to hear fire engines coming up the hill.

And, like most older brothers, he was very good to me many times. The most dramatic instance of his taking care of me occurred one day when I was three. A former maid who bore a grudge against my family came up to our house with an open razor in her hand. When my brother saw her, he grabbed me and hid me behind some sandbags in the garage until my father had talked to the woman and settled her complaints.

Although I have forgotten most of what went on during my preschool days in California, I do remember being frightened by that fire in the woods. Fire engines, with their lights flashing and sirens screaming, roared up the hill. The thick smoke hanging in the air hurt my nose and eyes and darkened the afternoon. Everyone in the household was in a panic as new blazes flared up, crackling in unexpected parts of the woods. Once a blaze burst out so close to the house that the firemen fought it with water pumped out of the swimming pool.

In Marin County I sometimes found relief from family tensions in the company of a man named Frank Haggerty. He was a combination chauffeur and nurse to my great aunt who lived nearby. He had had a good deal of medical experience, and, at the time my stuttering began, he was the only person in or near the family who held any hope for my improvement. "He will work out of this, don't worry. I've known others," he said to my parents, who were grateful for any encouragement.

Mr. Haggerty used to take me out on walks on the paths that wound around the hills behind our summer home. He would look up at the clouds overhead and ask me what I saw in their shapes. "Now tell me, do you think that looks like a dog?" he would ask. "Or a lady's face? What do you see?" I was very fond of Mr. Haggerty and remember always feeling secure when I was with him.

On other occasions, Annabelle, a special friend, would share with me in pleasant, communicative ways. She, too, was one of the pillars upon whom I could lean.

■ ─────────────────────────────────────── ■

My happiest childhood memories are of family trips, in which we were somewhat able to get away from the strains at home. Some of these were as short as the trip to Yosemite, but others were considerably longer. Before I started second grade, I had crossed the country by train and been shown around the Harvard University campus by a kind old Massachusetts doctor, a family friend.

We returned by water via the Panama Canal. What a wonderful experience that was! I was thrilled by the smoothness of the great ship as we glided through a channel that might have been sliced out of those steep hills by a giant's spade. It was fascinating to see in action the lock system which carried the ship up and down. And I remember thick jungle vegetation that reached out toward us on both sides, noisy with brilliant birds.

Three years after the Panama Canal trip, we all went by ship to Hawaii. I will never forget standing with my family on the ship's deck the night we sailed from Honolulu, leis of carnations and ginger flowers around our necks, listening to the Royal Hawaiian Band serenade our departure. A Hawaiian woman with a strong, rich voice sang the "Aloha" song, and then, as the ship began to move, we tossed our leis into the water, hoping that they would float toward the shore—a sign that we would return. Tears flowed from our eyes, and at that moment we felt especially united as a family.

■ ─────────────────────────────────────── ■

During the years just after my stuttering began, it seemed to have been mostly of the tonic type, in which a stutterer has stoppages in his speech, blocks in which he is completely stalled. A *tonic* block on the first letter of the word "five" might be written "f--------ive," while a *clonic*, or repetitive, block on that word would be written "f-f-f-f-five." I have seen a silent home movie, made before I started school, in which I am speaking and pointing toward a squirrel up a tree. My lips are moving, but tonic blocks are apparent. Every time they occur, my lips stay frozen in one posture for two or three seconds before the movement for the next sound begins.

In the movie these blocks appear to be severe ones. Various individuals have told me that they were both frequent and severe. However, it was not until I was almost five years old that I realized I had a speech problem. This realization came by degrees. Gradually I came to understand that there was something wrong with me. First, it was only a slight awareness that I was different from other children. Finally, my family's embarrassment, which I came to sense, and their frequent corrections made clear what part of me was lacking. I began consciously to try not to stutter.

■ ── ■

If my mother had answered the woman on the boat, she could have said that, yes, she and my father had looked for help for me. When I was five, she took me to one of the best known authorities on speech correction at that time, Mabel Farrington Gifford (now deceased).

Mrs. Gifford was the director of speech correction for the state of California. She herself had been locked in a struggle with stuttering until she was twenty-seven years old. When she was in her late teens and early twenties, she had gone for help to several stuttering schools, now called speech pathology centers, in the United States. One particularly famous school was in Buffalo, New York. There Mrs. Gifford found some relief, but she did not improve significantly until she went to Europe to study with prominent psychiatrists and at schools of suggestion, such as Coué's famous school of autosuggestion in Nancy, France. She was convinced that there was a substantial psychological factor in the problem and that real headway could not be made by concentrating on the mechanical aspects of stuttering alone.

In San Francisco Mrs. Gifford maintained a studio where she and several assistants conducted therapy sessions. When we met her, she must have been about fifty. She was a handsome woman with an extraordinarily calm air. Her studio rooms were furnished with beautiful rugs, tables, and chairs, and on the walls were hung paintings of peaceful scenes.

When my mother first took me to see her, Mrs. Gifford asked me to sit on a couch beside her, and slowly and clearly, in what I was later to hear referred to as her "velvet" voice, she told me an Aesop fable about a fox and some grapes.

When she finished, she asked me to retell the story. Although she was evaluating my speech, I was only aware of the pleasant atmosphere all about me. I have no memory of how much I stuttered on that occasion, but I suppose it was considerable.

My mother must have been encouraged as we left Mrs. Gifford's studio. Perhaps more than most handicaps, stuttering is one in which both the afflicted and their families feel alone. The first promise of improvement and the first sharing of the burden, especially with someone who has stuttered badly and mastered it, are very welcome.

Unfortunately, when we arrived at the studio for our second visit, Mrs. Gifford was not there. One of her assistants told us that Mrs. Gifford was away lecturing, that she would not often be there, and that she had asked this assistant to work with me. With the aim of improving my breathing and my ability to relax, the therapist asked me to do some pretending. Among other things, I pretended that I was a rag doll, that I was blowing out candles on a birthday cake, and that I was exhausted after splitting a huge pile of logs.

We did not see Mrs. Gifford on the third visit either. From the start there had been something about the assistant that disturbed my mother. On this third visit, irritated by a question about my temper, my mother declared that we had an incompatibility problem, and she withdrew me from the program.

My parents next went for help to a Stanford psychologist, the late Dr. Lewis Terman. After they had described my stuttering to him, Dr. Terman said he would send one of his master's degree candidates to our house for regular sessions of play therapy. This therapy involved the therapist's playing games with the child, talking about the games, and generally being his friend. The theory behind it was that stuttering was purely a psychological phenomenon, and that if the therapist could build a calm, trusting relationship, one free of fear, the psychological upset causing the stuttering would subside, and the stuttering would disappear.

The student, whose name was Helen, was a pretty girl with lovely brown eyes. I was happy every minute of the time she was there. We made piers for toy ferryboats and pushed the boats across the carpet. Some of the ferryboats carried little wooden cars with spoked wheels. Helen pretended that one of the cars was her own. I was the ferryboat worker who called out the orders when we docked or pulled away.

Helen brought a small china dog whom she called Fifi. I talked for Fifi some of the time. Throughout these sessions, which occurred twice a week, I was completely relaxed. Helen made me feel loved and wanted. She was my favorite playmate and my link with the outside world.

After a year of this therapy, my parents thought that my stuttering was as bad as ever, and, disappointed, they asked Helen to stop. Years later, when I was a student at Stanford and she was a faculty wife there, Helen told me that at the time of her visits the atmosphere in our house was so emotional and so negative she would have been surprised if my speech *had* improved. In another environment, she said, my speech might have improved rapidly. I rather think she was right. Removal of perpetuating factors can beneficially affect an organically based problem.

But, I am also sure that my family did not knowingly do anything to hold me back. With the makeups that they had they did the best they could. Because they did not like my stuttering, they often suggested that I think what I was going to say before I spoke, that I slow down, or that I take a breath. I remember being praised for not stuttering, which, of course, implied that when I stuttered I was a bad boy. I know that my brother was fond of the notion that I could stop it if I wanted to. I don't blame him for thinking this—when he could hear me speaking fluently to dogs and cats, then stuttering terribly with human beings.

At the time she came to us, Helen was in her early twenties. My mother was in her forties and did not readily take advice, even from people experienced in their fields. She particularly distrusted psychologists and anything having to do with psychology; I have always been amazed that she agreed to calling Dr. Terman.

I do not know whether Helen tried to change the way my parents were handling me, but I believe they would not have effectively carried out suggestions such as "Show no concern when the child is having difficulty with speech," or "Keep the mood of the household as free as possible from conflict." My family lived in a conflict atmosphere much of the time.

The author at 32 months with his mother, age 37, and his brother Charles, age 12. The photograph was taken at Mirror Lake on the floor of the Valley of Yosemite National Park in June, 1928. This was three days before the author began to stutter violently.

2

Childhood Stuttering

We all speak stutteringly at times, when we are tired, upset, rushed, or confused. There is more of this normal stuttering in the speech of small children than there is in the speech of adults because the children are physically, intellectually, and emotionally in a developmental stage. The physical coordination necessary for speaking is acquired gradually. The motor skills involved are complicated ones. Children's vocabularies are often inadequate for what they want to say, and, since the speakers are just learning to use complex sentence forms, this makes the intellectual task of verbal expression especially hard.

Emotional stress is often present when children are speaking. Frequently they are hurried or interrupted or ignored. The extra difficulty involved in speaking *up* to an authority is something children know well. Dr. Joseph Sheehan of UCLA once observed that small children have to speak up to practically everybody they know.

Normal speech imperfections are usually most in evidence when children are three or four. At this time they may do a good deal of word repeating, and occasionally they may prolong word sounds. This is a natural stage in language development, and if individuals close to the child do not seem surprised or alarmed about the unusual number of repetitions or prolongations, the amount of imperfection, which speech pathologists call *disfluency*, in his speech will probably soon drop to a familiar level.

However, sometimes, especially when there is a family history of stuttering, adults will overreact when a child is going through this normal disfluency stage. The danger then is that, by making an issue of his repetitions and prolongations, the adults will make the child self-conscious about his speech and actually encourage the development of abnormal speech problems.

Real stuttering, or abnormal disfluency, also usually begins around three or four, about the time the child starts to speak in sentences. It usually begins with occasional simple repetitions and prolongations which gradually occur more and more frequently.

There are a number of ways in which real stuttering can often be distinguished from normal disfluency. The beginning stutterer may speak in irregular or jerky rhythms. Perhaps he will move from slow to rapid speech and back again. Normally disfluent youngsters usually maintain a more even tempo when they speak.

Both abnormal and normal disfluencies are characterized by repetitions and prolongations, although in abnormal cases the symptoms are excessive in frequency and duration. Abnormal speakers may repeat more than one syllable in a single word. Abnormal prolongations often last longer than one second.

The speech of young stutterers may contain gaps or pauses in the middle of words. Normally disfluent children may pause between words, but they rarely interrupt a word midway.

Another characteristic of childhood stuttering is its cyclical nature. Except for consistently severe cases, the child will have periods in which he stutters considerably, alternating with ones in which his speech is relatively normal. These periods may be made up of days, or, more commonly, they may be several weeks long. The disfluency of normal speakers rarely occurs in pronounced cycles.

A small stutterer may show signs of struggle or tension when he speaks. A normally disfluent speaker will show no strain. Occasionally a stutterer's mouth will take an inappropriate, even grotesque, shape as he tries to speak. Normal speakers will not do this. Involved in his internal struggle, a stuttering child will sometimes look away from his listener, while a normal speaker, at disfluent moments, will usually not look away.

These are not all the differentiating symptoms, but they are the most common ones. Parents who are not sure if their child is showing true stuttering symptoms can ask a speech pathologist or a speech therapist to observe the child's speech and make a diagnosis. Professional help can be found by calling a local doctor or medical society, a local health department, or a nearby college or university which offers courses in speech disorders.

An excellent way to find qualified help is by writing the Stuttering Foundation of America at P.O. Box 11749, Memphis, Tennessee 38111-0749, or by calling their toll-free number, 1-800-992-9392 or 901-452-7343. The Foundation has a nationwide resource/referral list to speech pathologists who specialize in stuttering as well as fifteen books and informative brochures on stuttering. Mr. Malcolm Fraser, founder of this helpful organization and himself a stutterer, has a keen appreciation of stuttering and has contributed greatly toward a better understanding of it.

You may also wish to call or write the American Speech-Language-Hearing Association headquarters at 10801 Rockville Pike, Rockville, Maryland 20852. Therapists and pathologists who have been certified by this association can be found in most parts of the country and in many countries abroad. Each therapist has met a number of stringent requirements, including particular courses, substantial clincial experience, a master's degree, and a special examination.

A good therapist will know how to evaluate a child's speech without the child's recognizing what is happening. When a child is in the primary stage of stuttering, he probably does not yet know that he has a speech problem. He will be easier to help if he remains this way. Even though a child is in the primary stage, he can still stutter severely. Dr. Charles Van Riper, distinguished professor at Western Michigan University, has reported an instance in which a child repeated a word's initial syllable thirty-five times without realizing that anything was wrong. Tension and struggle symptoms at this primary stage may reflect only subconscious awareness; however, they may also be signals that conscious awareness is imminent.

Once a child knows that he stutters, he enters what is often called the secondary stage. His reaction to the discovery is frequently an emotional one, and his symptoms may become more complicated as he tries to suppress or to avoid stuttering. Sometimes his voice will rise in pitch, a symptom of interior tension. In the middle of prolongations his voice may begin to quaver, breaking the smoothness of the utterance and setting the stage for a host of extraneous and meaningless vocal sounds. Such behavior may be rapidly conditioned and become firmly implanted into the habitual pattern of stuttering, thus adding to it.

Another highly frustrating and feared symptom associated with secondary stuttering is involuntary shaking, or tremor. It can accompany clonic (repetitive) stuttering, and it is such a fast vibration of the lips, tongue, and jaw (eight or nine repetitions per second) that it cannot be accurately imitated by a normal speaker, or even by a stutterer who is momentarily free of speech interruptions.

In the middle of a sentence the secondary-level stutterer may stop speaking. He may be caught in a block, unable to bring forth a particular sound. He may be consciously trying to keep from stuttering on a specific word, or he may be afraid that stuttering is about to begin. Because of this generalized fear of stuttering, the youngster will start to speak less often when he is with other people. As Dr. Van Riper has written, "Stutterers are with us still. Usually as still as possible."

■ ——————————————————————————————————————— ■

The good news is that, in three out of four cases, real stuttering that begins in the child's third or fourth year will disappear by the seventh or eighth. Most of the time it does not stop dramatically. The cycles of bad speech become less severe, and they grow further and further apart. Slowly the stuttering fades away.

We are not sure why this happens. The late Dr. Robert West speculated that if we could understand what happens when this dwindling process occurs we might have an answer to the riddle of why stuttering begins. Perhaps there is at age seven or eight an end to a vulnerable or low-threshold period in the maturation process. Other chronic disorders such as asthma often disappear at this time.

■ ── ■

There are many things that family members can do to increase their child's chances of outgrowing stuttering. Efforts should be made to keep a small child in the primary stage, to avoid the complications that begin when a child tries not to stutter. However, it is important to understand that many secondary stutterers, as well as most primary stutterers, respond amazingly well to treatment that meets their special needs. Even if a child should turn out to be one for whom the problem continues, a supportive family environment can substantially reduce its negative effect on his life.

Parents sometimes respond to the development of a child's stuttering by wondering what they have done to him to make it happen. This question is probably unjustified; furthermore, when it does arise, it can influence parental behavior that will work against the child's improvement. Self-blame produces tension, and often anger. In a home these feelings add to a youngster's troubles, complicating his own emotions and increasing his stuttering. Any mistakes the parents made in the past probably were unintentional ones. Parents should realize that nothing can be done about past mistakes, ignore the temptation to punish themselves, and direct their energies toward learning all they can about the problem and instituting any changes in the home that will benefit their child.

■ ── ■

In 1953, when I was in the army and stationed in Japan, I often spent my free time visiting speech clinics to see what the Japanese were doing to help their stutterers. As I talked, often through an interpreter, to the therapists and pathologists in those clinics about the home lives of their patients, I learned that to be a stutterer in Japan was a disgrace. Even to have a stutterer in one's family was a shameful thing: Sometimes a family would try to hide a stutterer, to keep outsiders from knowing of his existence.

Later, on my way home from Japan, I encountered the same attitudes in India. In the United States at that time we had a more enlightened attitude toward the handicap, and since then I think our understanding of and tolerance for handicaps of all kinds have further improved. But because a young stutterer's self-concept, the way he thinks about himself, usually reflects the way his handicap is regarded in his home, family members should examine their own feelings about stuttering and consciously work toward the development of open, matter-of-fact attitudes toward the problem.

Parents who would never think of hiding a stuttering child may find that they are overprotecting him in ways that sometimes resemble hiding. For example, they may discourage him from answering the telephone or the door. There are usually mixed motives behind such prohibitions. The parents may be trying to keep their child from realizing the extent of his handicap. They may be trying to limit the number of failure situations he has to go through. But intertwined with the various motives may be a wish to spare themselves embarrassment or pain.

A small stutterer is more concerned about what his family thinks of him than he is about a stranger at the front door. He should not be forced into potentially difficult situations, but he should be allowed, within reason, to try any ordinary activity that he voluntarily responds to. It is possible that his parents' interfering with his doing something as normal as answering the phone or the door may raise or reinforce suspicions in his own mind about his abilities and the seriousness of his speech difficulties. On the other hand, unusually permissive treatment of a handicapped child can raise the same kinds of suspicions.

A child whose eyes have crossed needs extra help. He usually needs special glasses, and his parents must make sure he wears those glasses most of the time. They may also need to spend part of every day helping him with eye exercises. Beyond those special attentions, however, he will develop best if he is loved and disciplined exactly as the other children in his family are loved and disciplined.

A stuttering child also has special needs that his family should fill, but other than these requirements, he should be treated as normally as possible. Confidence fails and fears begin when a child starts to consider himself strange. His family must accept his stuttering as one characteristic of this child whom they love, and they must honestly feel that there is nothing about his stuttering to make them feel ashamed. Since such acceptance often follows understanding, it is helpful for family members to acquire at least a basic understanding of the disorder that has affected their child.

■ ─── ■

Parents of stutterers who are learning about the handicap for the first time usually begin with four questions: What is the relationship between stuttering and intelligence? What is physically wrong with my child? Is stuttering inherited? Can stuttering be cured?

These are reasonable questions for parents to ask, and I wish that they all had simple answers. Stuttering is a malady whose existence can be traced back to the time of man's first written records. Hippocrates and Aristotle wrote about stuttering, while in Roman times stutterers were nicknamed, "Balbus Blaesus," referring to their thick and stumbling tongues. In spite of the efforts of scientists to discover the origin of and a cure for stuttering, stuttering remains a controversial subject.

Only one of the four questions can be answered without qualification—the one about stuttering and intelligence. As a group, stutterers are neither brighter nor duller than normal speakers. In a large sampling of stutterers, there will be found the same range of IQ scores and other aptitude ratings as will be found in a large sampling of normal speakers. A stutterer may appear to be slow-witted when he avoids having to speak by saying "I don't know." I did that many times myself when I was young and unable to face the struggle involved in answering a complicated question. Usually I knew the answer perfectly well.

Also, the speech of mentally defective people is often rhythmically abnormal, full of pauses and repeating. A thoughtless association between abnormal speech and an abnormal mind might be easy to make; in the case of stutterers that association would be totally incorrect.

There is still no general agreement about the cause of stuttering. Some authorities believe that there is no physical difference between a stutterer and a normal speaker. They believe that stuttering is a symptom of a psychological problem, or that it is the result of inadequate or incorrect language development.

Many others, and I am one of them, believe that true stuttering does have an organic, or a physical, cause. We think that research to date supports the likelihood that the physical makeup of stutterers is slightly different from that of normal speakers. We think that stuttering is probably related in some way to the lack of a clear dominance over speech functions by one of the two cerebral hemispheres in the brain. Ordinarily, one of these hemispheres is in control; whereas, in certain individuals both centers may be struggling for dominance in sending nerve impulses to the paired speech muscles, so the timing synchronization that is automatic under normal dominance conditions easily breaks down. The stutterer may speak smoothly until he is confronted with some kind of stress, physical or psychological. His small margin of dominance gives his system only a fragile hold on the coordination necessary for normal speech. The signals become disorganized, or interrupted, and stuttering occurs.

There are also controversies about whether or not stuttering is inherited. Many stutterers have no known stuttering ancestors, or no stutterers close to them in the family line. In my case, I have been able to find only two fourth cousins who were stutterers. But research has shown indisputably that a family history of stuttering will be found much more often in the background of stutterers than in the background of normal speakers. Studies made by the late Dr. Bryng Bryngelson, formerly of the University of Minnesota, found stutterers to have relatives with the handicap eight times more often than normal speakers did. I have seen statistics from a genetic study of stuttering presently underway at Yale University that reinforce the earlier findings.

Scientists who deny the possibility of physical inheritance believe that families with stuttering experience are unusually sensitive to the appearance of any speech disfluency. As I previously indicated, members of such families are unusually quick to attach a label of stuttering to what may be normally disfluent speech. These authorities believe that the child accepts the label, reacts to it with self-conscious fear, and through attempts to suppress or avoid further disfluency, adopts speech behavior that becomes actual stuttering.

What stutterers and parents of stutterers need most to know about inheritance is that, while stutterers often have stuttering ancestors, there is no certain transmission of the handicap in any specific case. No one should be blamed for passing stuttering on.

Regarding a cure for stuttering, I do not want to shut the door entirely, but if "cure" means total disappearance of all stuttering symptoms for one's lifetime, I have to say that, except for the recoveries of the young children described earlier in this chapter, I have never seen a complete cure. However, I have seen countless instances in which individuals have learned to speak so smoothly that most of the people they know are not aware that they are stutterers. My own is such a case, although at one point in my life I stuttered on nearly every word.

■ ─── ■

We know that relatively small changes in family attitude or lessening of environmental strain can sometimes be enough to make a small child's stuttering disappear completely. The first thing that parents can do to help, then, is to examine their child's routine experiences carefully, trying to see them through his eyes, looking for sources of pressure or strain. Anything that makes life unpleasant for him and that is not essential should be eliminated. This process is sometimes called indirect therapy. It might also be called giving nature a chance. Many people have an appreciation of this and serve as fine models of its application.

In an earlier discussion of parent attitudes, I said that shielding or coddling a child may weaken him psychologically by making him think he is not able to function normally. Ordinary responsibilities and ordinary behavior requirements are essential for his normal development. However, parents often find that their child is regularly being exposed to unnecessary strains or frustrations which can easily be removed.

One way to locate areas of strain in a child's life is to watch for situations in which he regularly stutters. It is often possible to isolate the trouble-making elements in these situations. Sometimes a pattern of elements that is common to several of the situations can be found.

Records should be kept of words on which the child frequently stutters. There may be a common sound in these words that is physically or associatively hard for him. Secondary stutterers sometimes have difficulty saying words that begin with the sounds of "st." Often the meanings of the troublesome words will provide clues to problem subjects or situations.

This ongoing detective work may hold surprises. Perhaps no one has noticed that the youngster is present when older family members watch violent programs on television. A regular babysitter or a playmate may be responsible for unnecessary emotional or social tension. A weekly visit to a demanding relative may be given up, at least for a while. Perhaps it does not matter if the child's play clothes tear or get dirty. Perhaps his face and hands do not need to be scrubbed quite so often or quite so vigorously.

Because of the close relationship between physical condition and incidence of stuttering, it is important that the child be thoroughly examined by a physician and that if any problems are discovered that they be treated, and, if possible, corrected. I am sure that my own poor health as a child contributed to the maintenance and perpetuation of my stuttering. Most authorities believe that in childhood, at least, boys are neurologically less stable than girls. This may partially explain why male stutterers outnumber female stutterers, about five to one.

Parents should make sure that the child has a well-balanced diet and that he gets plenty of sleep. Stutterers seem to need more rest than normal speakers. Stuttering almost always increases with fatigue.

If there is any possibility that a small child has been encouraged to change handedness, to switch from using one hand to using the other most of the time, or if he seems to be ambidextrous, he should be examined by a neurologist to see which side is naturally the stronger one. In tests such as the Harris Test of Laterality and the Iowa Test of Lateral Dominance, a child is asked to do various things—to take a pencil and copy something, to shut one eye, to throw a ball, and so on. From the results, a neurologist can determine which hand is naturally dominant for the child. Related to cerebral dominance, this hand dominance seems to be a factor that is important in some stuttering cases, but not in all. It does not seem to have been applicable in mine.

However, there is a sufficiently high correlation between effective speech fluency and one-sidedness to make an investigation worthwhile whenever a child who is seven or younger has changed hands or is uncertain about preference. I have seen cases in which stuttering ceased after a small child began using the hand which was his natural one. With older children and with adults, an effort to change handedness has rarely resulted in improved speech. When there is improvement with an older stutterer, it is probably the temporary effect of the power of suggestion. After the age of seven, the child's stuttering seems to be so deeply embedded that a mere shift of dominance rarely produces noticeable results.

Whatever tensions exist between family members should be resolved as much as possible. The atmosphere in the home should be a loving one. Communication between family members should be open, with negative as well as positive feelings freely expressed, so that undercurrents of bottled-up resentment do not develop. If the child experiences a psychologically safe atmosphere around him at home, he will be better able to venture with confidence outside the home.

Since a relaxed and naturally quiet household will be beneficial for the child, household routines that affect him should be simplified and slowed down. Lively adults and older children often forget that continual noise and activity in a house can make a small child nervous. Time should be taken for casual, comfortable expressions of affection. The child should feel loved and wanted.

It is helpful if family members remember that stuttering is not voluntary behavior. When the child stutters, he is speaking as well as he can at that moment. Dr. Bryngelson expressed it well when he said that the stutterer is performing according to the dictates of his organism. This, of course, is why it is important to modify the child's environment, to lighten the demands on his organism to the point where he can meet them comfortably, and where the stuttering that occurs when the strains are too great will lessen or will not occur at all.

His family should react to his stuttering unemotionally. Anxiety about his speech should not be expressed in his presence. As a rule, no one should hurry him, or finish his sentences for him, or suggest that he breathe differently or that he begin a sentence over again. Communicative stress should be lowered in every possible way. He should be asked fewer demanding questions. He should not be asked to speak when he is tired or tense. He should never be asked to recite in front of other people. The entire family should make a special effort to use good speech manners. No one, including the stutterer, should be ignored or interrupted when he is speaking.

Remembering that stuttering occurs in cycles, parents should encourage the child to speak during his more fluent periods. Parents should let him have extra opportunities to talk at those times. During periods when his stuttering is more severe, he should have fewer speech requirements.

If the child knows that he stutters, his parents should point out to him that everyone has occasional speech disfluencies. Normal disfluency might be remarked on when it occurs, as it does regularly in real life and on radio and television. Occasionally, family members might allow a little stuttering in their own speech.

Also, if the child knows that he stutters, the word "stuttering" should occasionally be used in the house as casually as references to the weather. When Dr. Sheehan was at The University of Iowa Speech Clinic, he used to refer to the "conspiracy of silence" which often develops around a stutterer. He said it is as though two people are facing each other, talking. There is a hippopotamus between them, but neither person mentions that it is there. The implication behind the silence is, of course, that stuttering is bad, and it leads to the stutterer's trying to suppress or repress his symptoms by avoiding certain words or situations that make him stutter. These avoidances become habitual very quickly, and they are extremely hard to undo.

The business of keeping a child from thinking his stuttering is something bad often becomes subtle. For example, because of the negative judgment implied, it is probably wise not to praise a child when he does not stutter. Instead, his parents might praise him when he handles speech easily, even though he may do it without perfect fluency.

Children imitate their parents' speaking patterns. Youngsters who stutter need speech models that are uncomplicated and clear. When parents speak to their child, their speech rates should be slow. Their vocabularies should be simple, as should their sentence structures. Sometimes parents can use self-talk in which they describe in slow, simple speech something that they are doing while the child watches and listens. Parallel talk, in which the parents talk about what the child is doing, is another way of effectively providing models of slow, easy speech.

A friend of mine in Denver, who was a slight stutterer himself and in whose family there were other stutterers, had a little girl who began to stutter when she was five. I knew her then, and I thought she was one of the most severe cases I had seen. Her parents did everything they could to reduce the pressures in her life and to make their home situation a positive one.

Her father described to me the way he spoke to her. If he was at the sink washing the dishes, he would say very slowly and clearly, "I'm wash-ing the dish-es. I put the dish down. Whe-re's the dish towel?" Without his asking her to do so, his daughter would imitate him, and often in these sessions, she did not stutter at all. The approach to speech was a very easy one. There was much relaxed and loving interaction in the home. The child's organism was not overtaxed, and eight months after this program began, her stuttering was gone.

A June, 1932, photo of the 60-foot pool and summer house at Ross, Marin County, California. Fred's mother, 41, and brother, 16, are seated.

3

School Days

When I was five I started school in a small kindergarten called Miss Kennedy's. Although the reactions of other people to my speech had made me realize that I had a problem, I went off confidently enough on the first day. I was stuttering pretty constantly then. My new playmates teased me about it on the playground, so when the school put on a play, I was glad to participate as the silent Indian who did not have to say a single word.

The playground teasing was rougher at the Grant Elementary School, my next institution of learning. I can remember eating by myself when the students all took their metal lunchboxes out to the schoolyard, and worrying about being ganged up on by some of the older boys who bullied me and called me "Stutter Cat."

In the Grant School classrooms I began immediately to have trouble with oral recitation and reading aloud. Waiting for my turn to answer a question was torture. By the time my turn came, I was so excited I could hardly think of the answer, and my speech almost always went totally out of control. Reading aloud when the other students were following the passage in our book was hardest of all, because then I had to say specific words at specific times, and I could not substitute easier words for words that were hard for me to say. As I struggled, it seemed to me that all the children in the classroom were laughing, although I am sure that many must have been sympathetic. The Grant School teachers responded to my stuttering the same way that my parents did most of the time at home, by giving it what used to be called the "warts treatment." If you don't acknowledge the existence of a problem, it may go away.

Early in elementary school I began to devise ways in which I could avoid stuttering in front of the class. At home I would pre-write recitations on the subjects we were studying, making sure that I didn't use words that usually gave me trouble. In school at recitation times I would often ask to go to the bathroom, sometimes pretending that I had a nosebleed, and then I would stay out of the classroom until I thought my turn to speak had passed. Sometimes I could get out of reading aloud by saying I had forgotten my glasses. In many ways my childhood speech troubles were compounded by general poor health—the worst illness was a paralyzing attack of meningitis-encephalitis which followed the mumps when I was eight years old. But, at the same time, I was grateful for the illnesses because they meant I could escape for a while the speech pressures that were always waiting for me at school.

A stutterer often forgets that normal speakers speak imperfectly—that they sometimes hesitate, fill gaps in their sentences with sounds of "um" or "ah," repeat syllables or whole words. Distressed over his own difficulties, the stutterer imagines that normal speech is perfect speech, and he sets wishful goals for himself that nobody actually attains. I began to do this while I was still in the early grades. The contrast between my speech ideal and my own turbulent utterings was so very great that much of the time, along with the speech problem, I struggled with additional burdens of fear and shame.

My personality, which was developing at this time, was affected by my efforts to hide my stuttering both in school and at home. As much as possible I tried to stay away from circumstances in which disaster was almost guaranteed, such as reading aloud. This avoiding behavior seemed at first rewarding, because as I spoke less, I stuttered less, and so I suffered less. But, of course, continually looking ahead for approaching speaking situations that I somehow had to get out of was exhausting.

There were positive things about my experience in the Grant School. On entering, I was immediately put in a speech correction program under therapists who had been trained by Mabel Farrington Gifford. I didn't mind a bit being taken out of class once a week to go to these sessions. Their forty-five-minute length seemed too short, and I would have been delighted if they had been held every day. I was happy that I was not alone, that I had a friend in the speech therapist, and that I had some hope that I could get over this thing.

There were several youngsters in the program. Most of the others had less severe problems than mine, but at least one was a worse stutterer than I. At the beginning of each session we were told to make ourselves comfortable in our chairs and to close our eyes. Then, in a soft voice, the therapist would ask us to imagine ourselves in a place where everything was peaceful and beautiful—a meadow, perhaps, or an orchard in the spring, or the bank of a mountain stream.

Having established ourselves in our lovely spots, we were asked to turn our attention to our toes. "Feel the muscles in your toes," said the therapist softly. "Feel how tense they are. Now relax those muscles. Concentrate, and let go, let go, let go. Now concentrate on the muscles in your feet. . . ."

When we had worked our way up to our lungs, we were told to listen to ourselves breathing and to feel the flow of air moving freely into our lungs and out again. The progressive releasing of muscular tension continued until, with our jaw muscles relaxed so that our mouths hung open, we were asked to breathe out, making one long sound such as "ohhhhhhhhhhhh."

Later, we learned to drone out syllables while exhaling, and then to say in a slow, breathy way sentences such as "I am relaxed. I am calm." "When I am calm, my speech flows freely." "There is nothing wrong with my speech." And, indeed, my speech was better under those circumstances.

At that time all the California public school speech therapists were using the Gifford technique because Mrs. Gifford was, as I have said, chief of the state speech correction program.

When Gifford-trained therapists worked with young children, they concentrated on relaxation. The theory behind their efforts was that stuttering is a symptom of nervous tension and that a stutterer's nervous tension is caused by his fear of stuttering. To put it more simply, a person stutters because he's nervous, and he's nervous because he stutters. The only way to break into this circular relationship is to eliminate tension by consciously relaxing the body and the mind. Once physical and emotional calm is established, speech will flow freely. The stutterer will discover that there is nothing wrong with his speech mechanism. He can prove this to himself any time he wants to by talking when he is relaxed and by following the five points of what Mrs. Gifford called her star.

The older elementary school speech pupils were taught about the star. Each of its points had a name. The names were "Body Relaxation," "Breathy Outpouring," "Pause Between Phrases," "Short Phrases," and "Passive Mouth Action." The points were clustered around a central principle called "Still Feeling Within." As we practiced each point's technique, we always remembered that attaining a "Still Feeling Within" was our most important goal.

By the time I was in the eighth grade at the Grant School, I had had three successive therapists, all trained under Mrs. Gifford. The therapy worked while I was in the speech class. It has long been recognized that stuttering decreases when the stutterer is relaxed. The element of distraction was also operating there. We were all concentrating so much on the mechanics of relaxation that we were distracted from thinking about our stuttering. And we knew that if we did falter, no one would laugh. It was a closed, safe situation.

The problem came in transferring that sense of safety into our lives at school and at home. While I had good experiences in those weekly sessions and enjoyed my friendships with the therapists and with the other youngsters there, I continued to stutter in regular school recitations, and my oral reading grew steadily worse as the years went by.

I was more frustrated and upset by my stuttering than I had ever been before, because of the contrast between my fluency in the speech class and my disfluency in regular classes. In the special sessions I could speak without stuttering, and I did not know why this would not carry over into the other areas of my life. I felt guilty because I thought I was letting my friend the therapist down.

As I look back on those days, I now feel the major weakness in the Gifford therapy, at least for young children, was that it tried to prevent the occurrence of stuttering. Whenever one of us started to stutter, the therapist would quickly interrupt, saying, "Now wait a moment. Let's get back to calm stillness. Shut your eyes, and think of a beautiful scene. . . ." The implication behind these interruptions was that stuttering was offensive, something that we were all working to get rid of. No matter how cheerful the therapy sessions were, that underlying attitude fed our already established anxieties and our revulsions regarding ourselves.

How ironic it is that at the very moments in which we were absorbing a philosophy that affirmed our self-disparaging feelings, we children felt the most secure! The invaluable part of the program was the way in which it provided a friendly refuge in what often seemed a desperately trying world. I always looked forward to being with the therapist and her class. All three therapists who came to the Grant School while I was there were intelligent, thoughtful people, eager to help their students in every way they could. They provided more than a refuge. They provided escape valves for many of our troubled feelings. I often wish that all young people, especially handicapped ones, had ready access to counselors as sensitive and as loving as these.

Once, when tempers had been flaring more than usual in my family, the therapist who was working with us at that time said to me, "Fred, you seem to be having extra trouble with your speech. Is something wrong at home?" Her friendly concern was exceedingly welcome. I shut the door and told her everything, to the last detail, that was bothering me. It was absolutely against my family's code to air problems to outsiders, but that talk was a relief. Keeping things bottled up and hidden usually makes more trouble somewhere, between individuals or in one's own thinking. I find now that if I let my problems circulate a bit through the environment it helps me keep a more realistic view of the world, and of myself in the world.

■ ─── ■

One of the most maddening aspects of the handicap is that the stutterer never knows ahead of time what his speech is going to be like in a particular situation. Remembering past experiences, the stutterer often can make a good guess, although there are always surprises, both pleasant and unpleasant ones.

When I was in the fifth grade, I was asked to play "The Stars and Stripes Forever" on the piano for a school assembly. The piece was a fairly easy one, which I had rehearsed often without making a mistake. But on the day of the assembly when I started to play, I realized that both of my hands were one note too high on the keyboard. I tried for a few measures to move down, with no luck. It was a weird "Stars and Stripes" that came out, somewhat right but mostly wrong. At last, defeated, I banged my hands flat on the keys, turned to the audience, said perfectly fluently, "I'm starting over!" and played the piece through correctly. Ordinarily, when I was caught in such frustrating circumstances, embarrassed in front of my peers, I would not have been able to say a word without stuttering.

In my last year of elementary school I was nominated to run for the office of school treasurer. The boy who nominated me was the person who was running against me. I suspect, since speeches would have to be made, that he thought he had insured his victory by making me his opponent. But, again, absolutely contrary to what I was sure would happen, I did not stutter in any of my campaign speeches. Both my opponent and I were surprised, and I won the election.

Then, I discovered that as school treasurer I would have to deliver an oral report on the state of our finances before the whole school. That was bad news, and, as the report day grew near, my pessimism deepened because I was going to have to say that we had eighty-eight dollars in the treasury, and "eight" was one of the words I always blocked on.

The day before the report I thought of a solution. I added two dollars of my own money to the fund. I really wanted to carry off the report without stuttering, so I did everything I could to make that likely. I wrote out my short speech, avoiding all words that had made me even hesitate in the past. I said the speech over several times. And, on the morning of the report, I put on my blue-and-white good luck socks, socks that I had been wearing on the campaign speech days.

I felt hopeful as I walked out onto the school auditorium stage. Since my speech was not the first in the program, I joined some other students who were sitting on the stage in a row. As I waited, I mentally went over the five points of Mrs. Gifford's star, trying to establish the "Still Feeling Within" me. When my turn came, I took my time getting set at the podium, adjusting the microphone, aware of the big room filled with faces looking up. Then I took a deep breath and started in.

The first part of my report had to do with a Red Cross drive that had taken place the week before. I blocked severely on the "R" in "Red," and from then on everything was downhill. I stumbled on one word after another until, at the very end of the speech, when I was announcing the treasury total, I blocked on "ninety." I was two dollars poorer for nothing.

At every age, and at every level of difficulty or improvement, a stutterer must accept that he cannot know for sure whether or not he will stutter on any word at any time. This inconsistency is very hard to accept. At one point the stutterer, surprised by fluency in usually difficult circumstances, may be tempted to think about recovery; at another, shaken by failure where none was expected, he may be tempted to despair.

As the stutterer's unexpected stuttering becomes less important and less upsetting, he will relax, and, as I learned from Mrs. Gifford's therapy, his being relaxed will probably cause his stuttering to occur less often and to be less severe.

Even today I occasionally stutter unexpectedly. A noted authority on stuttering has said he thinks it will be interesting if, on his own deathbed, he is able to manage a fluent "farewell, dear world." All a stutterer can do is to maintain a sense of humor and refuse to make an association between fluency and personal success.

Mrs. Gifford, age 38, who helped the author in his childhood years.

4

Telephoning

When I was small, my experiences with the telephone were so calamitous that my parents forbad my using it; however, when I was halfway through elementary school, they decided that it would be therapeutic for me not only to make all my own calls but also to answer the phone every time I was conveniently near it when it rang. Like many stutterers, I dreaded using the telephone, and so I immediately extended my network of avoidance maneuvers to include the phone at home.

At that time we had a maid, a good-natured, distinctly overweight woman, who wanted me to call her Sweet Lamb. Sweet Lamb had an unusual, loose way of speaking—"garbled" is probably the most accurate adjective—and she loved to talk. I didn't love to talk, especially on the phone, so I made Sweet Lamb my interpreter. Sometimes I would be midway through a phone conversation, trying to get a homework assignment or making an arrangement to meet a friend somewhere, and I would go into so severe a block that I'd have to call Sweet Lamb from the kitchen to come and help me.

Smiling with confidence and anticipation, she would hurry into the hall where the phone was, and I would try to give her the message that needed transmitting, while the person on the other end of the phone line waited. Sweet Lamb did the best she could for me, but her speech was in many ways harder to understand than mine, and often information was lost or, worse, misunderstood. Once a friend who had called to ask about schoolwork talked to me through Sweet Lamb and then hung up and did the wrong assignment.

Sunday evenings were always difficult because that was when my friends in the neighborhood called to talk about which of our fathers would drive us to school the following week. I could spend all Sunday afternoon with several of those boys, talking fairly easily with them, but then the prospect of having to speak to them over the phone that night would give me indigestion during supper. I would look for an excuse to leave the house as soon as the meal was over and to stay away until I was sure the call had come, one of my parents had answered, and the weekly car pool decision had been made.

One morning I was eating breakfast alone when the phone rang. I suddenly thought of the Greek orator, Demosthenes, who tried to cure his own stuttering by filling his mouth with pebbles and then, standing on the Aegean shore, shouting his orations through the pebbles to the waves. No pebbles were handy, so I stuffed my mouth with toast before lifting the receiver. A second later, my mother answered the call on the upstairs extension. Later I heard her tell my father about a conversation involving a drunk that had somehow been transmitted onto our phone line.

In the spring of my eighth-grade year, an announcement came in the mail describing a two-week stay at a Boy Scout camp in the mountains. I was thrilled when I read about the riding, the swimming, and the hiking. I showed the paper to my parents, and they said that I could go. There was only one hitch. We were in our Marin County home when the announcement came. Before I could be accepted, the scoutmaster in San Francisco had to have a letter from our San Francisco doctor saying I was in good health. The notice was late in reaching us, having been forwarded to our summer home from San Francisco, and the deadline for the doctor's letter was two days away.

My mother suggested I call the doctor and ask him to send the letter right off. As usual, the mention of the telephone sent shockwaves through my stomach and my shoulders, but I wanted badly to go to that camp. I could not call on Sweet Lamb because she was in San Francisco. I was determined to force myself to make the call.

In those days there were no dial phones in rural areas. When we picked up the telephone receiver, an operator would come on and ask the number of the person we were calling. I wrote out the doctor's number on a piece of paper and then went off by myself to practice saying it. When I was alone, it was easy. I waited until everyone in the family either was out of the house or was downstairs and occupied. I was actually sweating with fear as I went to the upstairs phone and lifted the receiver. There was a click. An operator said, "Number, please." I opened my mouth and tried with all my will to say the number, but not a sound came out. The operator said, "Number, please," again, and I strained, red-faced, but the only sounds I could get out of my mouth were a few strangled gurglings. Twice more the operator said, "Number, please," and then I hung up.

During the next half hour I tried three more times to place that call. On the fourth try I finally said the number. The phone rang on the other end, and the nurse answered, "Good afternoon, Dr. Shaw's office." A new wave of devastating fear seized me, and, again, I was unable to utter a sound. I hung up, went downstairs and outside to the back of the house, and cried. Later in the day, when my mother asked about the doctor's note, I said I had decided not to go to camp after all.

It is hard for normal speakers to understand the telephone agonies that many stutterers go through. At the heart of the problem is the same communication pressure which exists in reading aloud in school, that of having to say specific words at specific times. The word "hello" is not particularly hard to say, but it is hard for a stutterer to say when he answers a phone, because he knows he must get it out immediately or the person on the other end of the line will hang up. In many cases, "hello" has become what we call a cue, something that reminds us of earlier bad experiences so powerfully that whenever it appears it automatically sets off waves of anxiety. It amuses me now to hear groups of stutterers discussing the difficulty of saying "hello" in introductions or over the telephone. Usually they have considered all sorts of dodges, such as "yes?" or "ummm?," or their own phone numbers, which sounds rather official, or their own names. I am very much aware that stutterers whose speech has improved are frequently scornful of such avoidances.

Actually, it is usually harder to say one's own name than it is to say "hello." Not only is there the problem of having to say the name quickly at a time largely determined by the listener, but one's name carries a heavy self-concept psychological load. It identifies one. It represents the whole person—all of the ideas that others have about him, as well as all of his own self-concepts. The handicap is such a frustrating and often humiliating one that most stutterers' self-concepts are somewhat tattered, if not really torn. In addition, there is virtually no possibility of substituting another name for one's own name. Of all the words in a person's vocabulary, his name is representative of something he should know and utter with unhesitating automaticity. To do otherwise implies all sorts of possibilities, none of them associated with normality. Since most stutterers have innumerable failures trying to say their own names, their names as cue words acquire immense compulsive force.

Specific word pressure and time pressure are also present in most telephone conversations. People usually make calls in order to get precise information, asking questions that require definite answers. And, of course, if the call is a long distance one, financial considerations intensify the pressure of time. On one memorable afternoon when I was twelve, I took five minutes to accept a party invitation.

When using the telephone, a stutterer is forced to communicate, relying on his voice alone. Whatever facial or body gestures he ordinarily depends on to help himself along are no good when he is involved in a phone call.

The phone is a link to the outside world. Many communicative variables filter through it. Most stutterers find it especially hard to speak to a stranger over the phone. Usually in such calls there is an extra concentration of necessary specifics. For instance, if I call a television repairman about my off-kilter set, I have to say what seems to be wrong with the set, what my name and address are, how he can find my house, what time and what day I would like him to come.

As a youngster I was more negatively conditioned to the phone than most stutterers, but, even in my worst periods, I had a few friends with whom I could talk over the phone moderately well. Paul was such a friend. Since calling a person I didn't know was a terrifying challenge, I would call Paul first and chit-chat with him for a bit. Then, using that momentum, I would hang up and quickly place the call to the stranger. Sometimes it worked.

Stutterers are notorious for having difficulty with telephone operators. To this day, if an operator cuts in and asks my phone number, I will occasionally stutter lightly on the figure "8" in my number's prefix, "868." On very rare occasions I have found myself using the last-ditch possibility of saying three sound-alike words, such as "hate-sick-sate," thus enabling us to get the billing arrangements out of the way and to get on with the call. I am well aware of this being an avoidance maneuver that is not to be condoned.

However, when I think about stutterers and telephone operators, I always remember a day in 1946 when I was a college student visiting a friend in New York City. I had to give a phone number to a New York City hotel operator. After the operator had come on the line and had said, "Number, please," "Gramercy," the word exchange in the number, simply stuck in my throat. It was a bad block; I kept trying and trying, but the only sound I could make was a faint croak. The operator must have heard it because suddenly she said, "Sir, I know what your difficulty is. Now, I have plenty of time. You just relax and say the number when you can." She said it in the nicest way, and in a moment I was able to say easily "Gramercy," the number, and "Thank you."

5

Complications

Even though I had been stuttering for two years when I started kindergarten at Miss Kennedy's, I had not up to then thought much about my speech. During my elementary school years, my awareness and my dread of stuttering grew. By the time I reached the eighth grade the problem was on my mind much of the time, and I had developed negative attitudes toward most areas of my life that were connected with speech. The ploys that I thought up to avoid stuttering, often by avoiding speaking altogether, were constantly increasing in number and in complexity, since each bad episode produced a new word or a new set of circumstances to watch out for in the future.

Although my troubles were actually mounting, at the time I reached junior high school my speech seemed to have improved. I was very proud of this, even though I knew that my stuttering was decreasing only because my avoidance schemes were working. I was becoming, in part, what we speech pathologists call an "interiorized" stutterer. In his book, *The Nature of Stuttering*, Dr. Van Riper describes the interiorized stutterer as ". . . one who is able to conceal the overt manifestations of the disorder though at the price of constant vigilance, avoidance, and anxiety." The price was high. Avoiding speaking, or getting through speaking situations without having to say any feared words, required so much inventive alertness, and used up so much psychic energy, that at the end of most days I was exhausted. I also paid a price by allowing the boundaries of my world to shrink, as fear of stuttering in response to unfamiliar surroundings made me refuse one new experience after another.

Typical of my anxious, avoidance-oriented behavior at that time was my choosing to go to a junior high school for the ninth grade, instead of going straight on to the regular high school. I was apprehensive about any change, and I thought a step to junior high would be only half as big as one to high school, and, therefore, that it would be only half as hard to make. Going to Marina Junior High School was a mistake. My friends went on to Lowell High, and I had a difficult year without them.

Earlier that summer I had heard my father saying to a friend that he and my mother thought I should go into engineering, because in that field I would not have to depend on my speech to a large extent. While he meant to help me, I was enraged at what seemed to me a derogatory statement. I considered myself inferior to normal speakers, but I could not stand the thought of *other* people's looking at me that way. And so, in a fit of pointless rebellion, I enrolled in an art course instead of algebra, because algebra suddenly stood for acceptance of engineering and my father's disparagement. In the middle of all my surging, miserable emotions, there was a grain of stubbornness that refused to accept as inevitable the tag of cripple.

As soon as he learned that I had not signed up for algebra, my father called the principal, and my second day at Marina began with a triple-threat half hour in the principal's office where he sat and watched me as I used his telephone and tried to tell my father why I had picked the art course. I got halfway through the first word of my first sentence and stayed there, repeating one syllable for the remainder of the "conversation." After I hung up, I told the principal that I would take algebra the following year.

At the beginning of the second semester, we changed English classes. My new teacher passed out textbooks and asked each student to say his name and his book's number as she went down the rows. I stuttered when my turn came. The teacher, whose name was Miss Fielding, gave me a measuring look and asked me to speak to her after class.

After the bell rang and the others had left the room, she said that she wanted me to take her public speaking course because public speaking would help my stuttering. I didn't want to do it. A class devoted to talking was the last thing I needed! The class also met at the time of my art class. But I was not given a choice. Miss Fielding arranged for my enrollment, rearranged my schedule, and told me to be in the public speaking room at class time the next day.

I suppose the reason the teachers back in the Grant School had paid little attention to their students' speech problems was that there was a speech correction program in operation at the school. At that time in California, public school speech therapy was almost entirely concentrated in the elementary schools. I would not see a trained therapist again until I went to college. Many of the junior high and high school teachers must have recognized their adolescent students' continuing need for therapy, and some of them decided to help us on their own.

I was the only person in the public speaking course who was not a normal speaker. I craved normal speech for myself. I fantasized about it. I equated normal speech with social acceptability and power, and I felt my handicap to be extreme. Having to stand up and speak in front of that group was always embarrassing, and the difficulties were heightened by

Miss Fielding's habit of calling out advice to me in front of the whole class, the same old useless advice I had heard all my life: "Slow down, Fred!" "Take your time!" "Take a big breath, Fred!" "Think what you're going to say before you say it!" My stomach was upset every time I spoke.

As the semester went by, my stuttering increased markedly because my avoidance strategies could not keep up with the barrage of failures that I encountered in that class. In my speeches, my vocabulary and my sentence structures became unnatural to the point of being unintelligible as I tried to avoid feared words and still do the weekly assignments. There were suddenly more words to avoid than I had substitutions for. It was like a grass fire out of control.

As my stuttering grew worse, any degree of pride that I had felt at the beginning of the year dissolved. The feeling of being somewhat adequate socially, which I had earned for myself with effort and vigilance, slipped away again, and I blamed Miss Fielding and her class for that loss. My chief means of protecting myself was eroding away, and with it was disappearing my psychological security.

As its final exam at the end of that year, in June of 1940, the public speaking class went to the school auditorium to deliver prepared speeches from the stage. We had not used that room before. Our assignment was to speak for or against the United States' placing an embargo on trade with Japan. I had been told to write a "con" paper, and I did my best to prepare a speech that listed all the advantages of maintaining trade and friendly relations, using mainly words on which I had never, or rarely, stuttered before.

I did not sleep well the night before the final. As I sat the next day with the others, a little group of twenty, in the front rows of an auditorium designed to hold a thousand, I remembered my eighth-grade treasurer's report in the little Grant School auditorium and wondered how I had ever thought I could get through it.

The first speeches began. As usual, I was afraid and my stomach was aching. All of a sudden I had a terrifying feeling of disaster. I felt as though I were losing myself. The room seemed to be floating, and the speakers' voices were far away. I noticed that my right leg was shaking. I tried to stop it by pressing down on it with both my hands, but my arms were weak. Miss Fielding was calling my name.

I got up slowly. My classmates' faces were blurs. Both my legs were now shaking, and I could not judge how much space there was between my feet and the floor. Somehow I got up the steps to the stage, turned, and blocked on the first syllable of my first word. Nothing would come. I tried forcing my breath out. I jerked my head from side to side, then up and down. I heard some nervous titters from the audience. I twisted my mouth around, stuck out my tongue, winced, and squinted my eyes. Still nothing could be heard except my strained gagging. My face was scarlet. I could hear far off in the distance, "Take your time, Fred. Take a breath."

I could not breathe. I thought I was losing consciousness, so I sat down on the dusty stage floor, my chest heaving as I tried to get my breath. Miss Fielding came up onto the stage and helped me back to a seat in the auditorium. I sat there in a state of the most intense anxiety I had ever known. I have no idea how long that anxiety lasted. I know that I felt some of it for days afterward, and I can feel it still when I remember it. Although I was fourteen years old when it happened, that is one of the two or three worst experiences of my life.

∎ ———————————————————————————————— ∎

During my junior high and senior high school years, I developed certain ideas about stutterers and normal speakers. Some of these beliefs continued well into college, and a few of them stayed with me even longer.

I was obsessed with what I did not have, and that was normal speech. I did not hear disfluency in the speech of the normal speakers around me, and I did not notice much that was not going well for them. Their lives seemed perfect to me, and I thought that mine would be perfect also, if only I could get this stuttering out of the way. I had a good bit of what Dr. Sheehan has called a "giant in chains complex"; I thought my hidden potential would be realized immediately if my stuttering could be stopped.

Part of this mistaken thinking was simply the result of my being young. Often it is not until individuals are in their late twenties that they understand that the important accomplishments in life are achieved slowly, with many errors, backtracking, and further learning along the way.

While it is easy to be sympathetic about a handicap that is so highly visible and so constantly frustrating as this one, we speech pathologists who work with stutterers have to help them see how little their stuttering actually interferes with their doing what they want to in the world. They find that they cannot blame their stuttering for their lack of achievement nearly so much as they thought they could. So far as most of their endeavors go, they must recognize what Dr. Sheehan was expressing when he said, "Your stuttering does not hurt you, and your fluency does you no good.

One result of my overvaluing normal speech was my feeling unreasonably proud about the times when I did speak without stuttering. Many stutterers share this attitude and will go to any lengths to conceal from others the fact that they stutter. There is great fear of losing face, or of not being able to live up to the idolized, imagined self. My pride in my apparently improved speech as I began junior high school was this kind of pride. It was a precarious balancing act that I was performing, in which almost any complication could knock me down. Miss Fielding's public speaking class did just that, but as soon as I got away from her, I began setting up my balancing act again.

At that time I did not know anyone who could set me straight about the value of normal speech. Every day I was embarrassed by my lack of it, and, because I was preoccupied with my troubles and alone a good deal, I used to make up fantasies about being a masterly orator who could hold huge audiences spellbound. I would imagine myself very strong, totally in charge, molding and commanding crowds of listeners who could not resist my persuasive powers. A bomb could not make me stutter. My whole being would flow forth in fluent, dynamic phrasing. I had no fear of speaking—all I had to do was to step out and make myself known.

These thoughts were similar to ones that every young stutterer has had, and, under normal conditions, when the person spends only a moderate amount of his time pursuing such ideas, he finds they can provide comfort and relief from the pressures of everyday reality. But, when a person spends too much of his time on such thoughts, the thoughts begin to interfere with his being able to develop the skills and attitudes that are necessary for survival in the real world. To get along, stutterers must see things as they are.

The other harmful consequence of my fantasizing about being an orator was that it encouraged my ideas about the importance of absolutely perfect speech. Many stuttering complications evolve when a stutterer has an anxiety reaction to every small speech failure. Stutterers who are unreasonably perfectionistic about their speech often develop compulsive behaviors that become roadblocks in their journey toward improvement.

Similar to fantasy were thoughts that I often had about magic. There was the superstitious kind of hope for magic that made me, when I was very young, try to sit on certain good luck chairs when I had to talk at home. The blue-and-white socks that I wore for my eighth-grade treasurer's report turned out not to have magical powers after all. When I tried to not step on cracks in the sidewalk, it was not to save my mother's back, the superstition in the familiar children's rhyme. I did it to help me keep from stuttering in a particular conversation, to a particular friend, or on a particular occasion.

It was partly because I had experienced unexpected moments of fluency that I used to believe a larger, powerful magic really might appear to rub out my stuttering forever, as an eraser rubs out marks on a chalkboard. Or, a rare magic might come sweeping into one situation in which I was having a bad time, and that magic would keep my speech apparatus from collapsing. It might happen at the very last minute when I was facing a threat, such as having to speak to an audience or having to talk on the phone. Somehow, in the feared situation, magic could pull me through.

Again, these were the thoughts of a young person who had read and believed fairy tales when he was small. It was also childlike to imagine quick, total rightings of troublesome wrongs. But, this person who was fantasizing and hoping for magic had very little else to turn to. Therapy had not been lastingly helpful, he had no one with whom he could share his feelings, and he had absolutely no idea how he could constructively help himself out of a predicament that was almost continually intolerable.

6

To the Teacher

I have often wondered what it is about stuttering that makes listeners want to give advice. The on-again–off-again characteristic of the difficulty usually leads a listener into believing that it can be "turned off" at any time with little effort. Perhaps it is because the symptoms are so dramatic that they arouse unusual amounts of sympathy. The suggestions of my well-meaning junior high school teachers were repeated with variations by others teachers as I went on to Lowell High.

One English teacher thought the problem lay in my neck. My neck was too tense, she said. If I did certain neck relaxing exercises, which she demonstrated for me, my stuttering would likely disappear. I did the exercises and went on stuttering.

A history teacher told me that he had given me a C because I didn't recite enough in class. His expectation was that the more I recited in class, the less fearful I would be, and, eventually, the less I would stutter. I could have told him how this had worked with Miss Fielding, but instead, stuttering as much as ever, I recited more and got a B for the following quarter.

My tenth-grade Spanish teacher, Miss Constanza, thought that my stuttering could be corrected by the regulation of my diaphragm. Whenever I began to stutter in class, she stopped everything and walked up the row to my desk. After telling me to stand up and take a deep breath, she would put her hands on my rib cage and order me to exhale each word separately. She braced herself and then, as each word came out, she would give my ribs a strenuous push. In this manner she would pump me to the end of a sentence, as though I were a tire in need of air.

Despite this embarrassing therapy, Spanish was a subject that I liked, and I continued to take it throughout high school. About halfway through my junior year something happened in Spanish class that made me think my longed-for magic had occurred. Miss Constanza was my teacher again. She brought in a play for us to read aloud in class. We were all assigned parts, and when it came time for me to read my part I did it with fluency. Miss Constanza dropped her book on the floor and shrieked, "Alleluia!" Everybody in the class was startled, and rather excited for me.

It took two weeks for the class to get through the play. Every time my turn came I read with almost complete fluency. I'm sure Miss Constanza thought her diaphragm-pumping had paid off at last.

When the play was finished, we were given a novel which, like the play, we were to read aloud. When my first turn came, I blocked early in my first sentence, and from that moment everything was just as it had been before the play.

■ ── ■

We know that stutterers will often speak better when they take on a role that is different from their everyday one. When we started to read the Spanish play, I became Roberto, but, when we went on to the novel, I turned back into Fred. As Roberto I must have become immune to many of the words and situations that normally functioned as fear cues for Fred.

Stutterers sometimes speak better in plays than they do ordinarily because they know that the world in which they are speaking is not real. The consequences of their words and actions are limited to the imaginative life of the play. Threats and debts in drama may be temporarily frightening, but both the actors and the audience know that this is make-believe, that in half an hour or so when the play is over, any danger it has contained will disappear.

Often a stutterer will find that his speech changes when he changes roles in actual life. The famous preacher, Charles Kingsley, said that he never stuttered from the pulpit, but that he did stutter badly when he met members of his congregation and other people in everyday surroundings. Like Kingsley, some stutterers function best when they are in positions of authority. They may feel most assured when they are entirely in control of the situation, able to say what they want to when they want to, free from the pressures of being interrupted or of having to answer questions.

The effect of a role change is usually a change in one's feelings of adequacy. It can work more than one way, of course, but, when a stutterer's speech improves after a role change, it almost always means that he feels more competent in his new role. It is possible that my surprising fluency when I was running for the position of school treasurer in the eighth grade was partly the result of a role change which increased my feelings of adequacy. I had never been a candidate for office before.

There are many degrees and kinds of role changes that may affect a stutterer's fluency. A rather dramatic one occurred in 1972 when I was on a ship bound for Australia, about to cross the equator. The ship's social director had organized the presentation of a traditional ceremony. She asked me to play the part of the prosecutor in King Neptune's court. I was apprehensive because it meant having to read aloud from a long script, and I knew from other voyages that almost everyone on board would be listening, some hanging from the balconies of the upper decks, others sitting in rows on the main deck. However, I put on my costume of robes and hat and beard, and went off by myself to develop an appropriate voice for the part—one a little deeper than my own, more melodic, more deliberate and confident-sounding. I'm sure both the costume and the new voice contributed to my feeling, once I began to speak in the actual ceremony, that I really was the prosecutor. I found I was having a wonderful time, booming away in rolling rhythms, with no signs of stuttering at all.

■ ─── ■

I wish I could tell Miss Constanza about role changes; she would be interested in the solution to the mystery of Roberto's fluency. I think most of my junior high and high school teachers would have been glad to have been given a synopsis of what we now know about stuttering. Miss Fielding's directions were the commonest wrong ones, typical of suggestions made by kind teachers everywhere who do not understand the disorder. Because this well-meant, instinctive instruction often happens to be precisely what a young stutterer should not receive, it is important that teachers who have stutterers in their classrooms learn from professionals what they should do.

The degree to which a youngster will stutter at any one moment is closely related to his feelings about himself at that moment. In school, where social pressures are usually greater than they are at home, the attitudes of his classmates and his teachers toward him and his affliction will have much to do with how well he can perform.

Teachers' attitudes are important, both in the way they affect the general class atmosphere and in the way a teacher responds to the special problems that having a stuttering student presents. I have seen case histories in which a young person's stuttering varied markedly from one year to another as he advanced in school with the same classmates, his fluency reflecting the sympathetic or the not-so-sympathetic natures of his successive teachers.

If the teacher realizes that when the student stutters he is speaking as well as he can, that he is stuttering because the demands that are being made on his mechanism are exceeding his ability to cope with them, it becomes clear that the best way to help him is to lighten those demands.

Urging a young stutterer in the middle of an attack to slow down, to breathe deeply, to think of substitute words, or to wait and to think what he wants to say and then to try again—all these increase the tension that the youngster feels. Having the teacher or another student say the word for him also adds to the strain. Sometimes the teacher or the student misunderstand his intention and will say the wrong word for him. Being singled out in ways that make him feel different and inferior to his fellow students aggravates the situation further. Behind the vigorous correcting is the unmistakable assumption that stuttering is unpleasant and wrong, something that everyone wants eliminated.

The teacher who wishes to modify the classroom environment in ways that will help the stutterer must first try to respond to his stuttering in an unemotional way. Sentimental sympathizing is humiliating. The student should be listened to patiently. He should not be hurried. He should not be interrupted.

Since many of a stuttering student's traumas involve oral recitation, the teacher might have a frank talk with him about how to handle speaking in class. The youngster should know that he is going to be allowed to speak when he wants to. It is usually very unwise to exclude a stutterer altogether from classroom speaking. Recitation should be put on a voluntary basis, the stutterer raising his hand or signaling in some other way when he wants to speak. An atmosphere of class discussion is usually much more comfortable for him than one of question and answer, since class discussion permits him to make his contributions in an inconspicuous way.

When question-and-answer periods must occur, it is often helpful if the teacher can arrange things so that the stutterer responds to questions requiring very short answers. Ordinarily, he will be able to manage "Yes," or "No," and, if he blocks on one of these words, he can always nod. Responding to questions will assure him that he is an active member of the class. If he finds he can manage short answers and gains confidence, the teacher might begin to try for slightly longer answers, but this should always be done slowly, and always in a casual way. Whenever an experiment does not work, it should be abandoned. It is best not to let a young stutterer continue to participate in activities in which he repeatedly fails.

A situation even more difficult for many stutterers than oral recitation is that of oral reading, a situation in which they are forced to perform competitively with normal-speaking students. The late Dr. Wendell Johnson once said this is like running a lame boy in the hundred-yard dash. The problem is compounded when every student is following the reading with his own copy of the text because then the stutterer is unable, through improvisation, to avoid especially difficult sounds or words. It will be the last straw for him if the teacher decides to have the students read in turn, seat by seat, and he is forced to sit there in a fit of anxiety, watching his trial inexorably approaching.

The teacher should give the stuttering student a chance to engage in verbal activities in which he can have some experience of success. Most stutterers can sing fluently. Sometimes stutterers become fluent when they are pretending to be other people, as I did in my high school Spanish play. Choral reading, in which several students read simultaneously, is easy for most stutterers. A student who usually stutters may speak more easily if he is allowed to talk about a favorite hobby or a favorite pastime.

In every one of these activities, the difference between "allowed" and "forced" is crucial. "Allowed" puts the student in a healthy, offensive position; "forced" establishes him, especially in his own mind, as defensive and, usually, doomed.

If the teacher knows that a stutterer is being mocked by other students, talking to the mockers about the affliction may help. Understanding often leads to compassion. In addition, normal-speaking students might be told that they can help their classmate by trying not to show any aversion they may feel toward his stuttering behavior. A stutterer who is being ridiculed should be advised to appear as nonchalant and indifferent as possible. Most teasing stops if the target is not visibly affected.

And, finally, if a relationship of friendly trust has been established between the teacher and the stutterer and if the stutterer is receiving no effective counseling elsewhere, the teacher may be able to act as a counselor for the stutterer, encouraging him to develop some of the sustaining attitudes and habits that I am going to describe in a discussion of counseling in Chapter 8.

Phobic Fear

Stutterers have contrived many more avoidance maneuvers than the few I have described in the preceding chapters. One of these maneuvers involves the use of humor—laughing instead of speaking, for example, or reacting to one's own poor speech in a clownish way. Or, a stutterer can avoid speaking by pretending he does not hear a question. Another common device is withdrawal, attempting to be inoffensive to the point of being socially invisible. Some stutterers develop an aversion to any kind of formal behavior. These people feel pressured whenever they have to conform to social rituals. Other stutterers, for whom formal behavior may have become automatic after much practice, feel safest when they are following these prescribed forms. For them, pressure mounts when they have to make the many behavioral choices that exist in informal situations. Some stutterers resort to gesturing, or to writing messages whenever they can.

Many avoidance maneuvers have been devised by stutterers in an effort to keep away from what speech pathologists refer to as "communicative pressure." The more restricted a stutterer is as to what he must say and when he must say it, the greater is the communicative loading in that situation for him. In avoiding, he is trying to arrange things so that the communicative initiative will be his—so that he can decide if he wants to speak, what he will say if he does want to speak, and how and when he will say it.

At the University of New Hampshire I am chairman of the Academic Policy Committee, which conducts its meetings according to *Robert's Rules of Order.* Because the parliamentary procedure is so restrictive, saying the words of the set questions and responses quickly is sometimes slightly difficult for me. I know it is not worth worrying about, and so I just relax and get through each of the forms as it comes along.

Communicative pressure also increases with the importance of the message. When it becomes severe, this pressure reminds me of the hot potato game that children play in which, once the "hot potato" has been thrown to a player, he tries to get rid of the object as quickly as he can.

The children's feigned terror about being burned resembles the trapped panic that many stutterers feel when a strong communication demand is thrown their way. The frantic impulse is to get away from it, to pass it on to someone else as quickly as possible.

This is why stutterers often speak more easily when they are on the edge of a direct line of communication. It is why a stutterer can contribute to an open group discussion more easily than he can say the same words in answer to a question that has been addressed to him alone. Conrad Wedberg, the author of *The Stutterer Speaks*, has told about being at a state fair where he saw a little boy tending a large hog. When Mr. Wedberg asked the boy how old the hog was, the boy went into a stuttering block and could not reply. Mr. Wedberg waited, and, after the spasm ended, the boy turned to the hog and said, "You know you're three years old." He was able to talk to Mr. Wedberg through the hog because the reply was not in the main channel of conversation and directed to a person.

■ ── ■

By the time I reached high school I was moving rapidly into the worst stage of my stuttering, a stage that was going to last for several years. I was so ashamed of my stuttering that I considered it unmentionable. I could not bring myself to speak about it, and it was rarely referred to in my home. I was determined to keep my stuttering hidden within myself as much as I possibly could, and so I began even more than I had before to maneuver to avoid communication pressure. Every time I failed and had to face a hard speech situation I would simply crumple.

When I had to read aloud or to answer definite questions in school, I stuttered badly, but in those situations in which I could volunteer to speak and could choose my own words, such as going to the board and writing with chalk, as I explained a mathematical problem, my speech was better.

Often my statements did not seem sensible because I was avoiding words that would make me stutter. At other times my thinking actually was muddled because I was concentrating on hindrance rather than on sense.

As for my relationships with my peers, except for a few close friends, I was convinced that my classmates thought of me either as a kind of court jester or, worse, as a pathetic figure who could only express himself in contorted sputters.

I did have fluency, more or less, with my family so long as there was no pressure in the situation. If the conversation at the dinner table became emotional, I might begin to block. I could have friends over and speak to them fairly well face to face. But the problem was acute with the telephone, especially when someone from my family was in the room with me or within earshot when I had to use it. My stuttering was always severe whenever I would have to introduce friends from the outside to members of my family.

Physically, along with acne, voice-changing, and the other embarrassing characteristics of male adolescence, I was trying to cope with increasing stomach pain. My nervous stomach condition worsened until in the middle of my sophomore year spasms of the duodenum began. Our doctor gave me drugs to relieve the spasms so that I could continue going to school.

At this time there were two major developments in my stuttering. Both were especially terrifying for a person who had been trying to suppress his stuttering through conscious control.

One change was physical. This was the appearance of tremors, the extremely fast vibration of the muscles near the mouth area, which I described briefly in Chapter 2. This violent shaking, broken periodically by even more violent jerking movements, frightens a stutterer into a state of blind panic because he cannot anticipate its beginning, and, once it has begun, it is involuntary. Sometimes he can interrupt a tremor by making a strong sudden movement of his head or chin—one explanation for a stutterer's grotesque facial gestures—but at other times such movements will have no effect. Occasionally the tremor will spread to other parts of the head or body. One of my earliest tremors was the shaking in my legs on the day of the ninth-grade public speaking final. Tremors make me think of a car that is running roughly after its ignition has been switched off. The driver can do nothing to stop it. He must sit there and endure the unpleasant shivers and jolting until the mechanism quiets down of its own accord.

The second change, a psychological complication, was my entering the "phobic stage" of stuttering. My phobia was an unreasonably intense fear of certain words and of certain speaking situations. I had been afraid of these for a long time, but never so persistently and so deeply afraid, or in such an uncontrollable way.

In 1911 a German authority named Alfred Appelt wrote that all severe stutterers know firsthand the meaning of the word, "dread." In the phobic stage, the feeling is that dread is flooding in and engulfing the helpless stutterer. As I did with tremors, I can describe the immobilizing effect of this phobic anxiety with an analogy in which the stutterer is the driver of a car that represents first his speech mechanism and then his entire body. When phobic fear first appears, the driver notices that he does not have much control over his car's braking. He has to pump the brake hard to get the car to slow down or to stop. Gradually, as the phobic state continues and the anxiety increases, the car's brakes respond less and less to the driver's pumping, until suddenly they won't work at all. Eventually, the driver is trapped in a defective car that is going the way it wants, as fast as it wants.

The severity of phobic fear varies, according to the condition of the individual and according to the situations he knows or imagines he is about to face. At its worst, it affects virtually everything he tries to do. Motor acts that he usually manages easily, such as tying his shoes, become difficult. He will speak and behave illogically because he is so distracted by his fear.

The effects of phobic fear are much harder for a stutterer to endure than the stuttering blocks themselves. When the phobic state takes over the stutterer's dreams, the dreams become terrible nightmares about stuttering. I often woke up to find my sheets were wet with sweat after one of those nightmares.

Much of what frightens a phobic stutterer never really happens. Immense amounts of psychic and physical energy are wasted. The stutterer is wild with apprehension, concocting all sorts of horrible situations that he might have to face, most of them beyond the realm of reality. He constantly searches his listeners' faces for signs of aversion to his stuttering. He is paranoid about finding or imagining negative reactions, making them unreasonably important, and adding them to his collection of neurotic preoccupations.

In this state, the stutterer is obsessed with his stuttering. He is a stutterer first and foremost—everything else is secondary. Life becomes narrowed down to what the speech will or will not allow, and the personality is molded within those walls.

8

Advice for Counselors

A child who has lived in a neurotic, tense environment is much more likely to develop phobias than one who has not. But, no matter what my home situation was like, I am sure I could have avoided all or most of this devastating stage if I had been guided during my high school years by a trained therapist, or by a school counselor who was informed about stuttering. A therapist, of course, would have recognized the beginning signs of a phobic condition and would have known what to do to check its development. But, even if I had been receiving no specialized help with my speech, a sensitive school counselor could have helped me keep some realistic perspective about my difficulties.

At the start it is often hard for a counselor to reach a stutterer of high school age, especially if the stutterer feels, as I did, that his handicap is so repellent he cannot stand to talk about it. However, cheerful rectitude and a sincere desire to help will usually prevail. No one wants to suffer alone. A stutterer who feels lost needs a good listener, and, as I discovered in elementary school, it is an enormous relief to share the burden with someone outside the circle in which one's conflicts are occurring. Cues multiply and fears spread the fastest when no one is available to guide a young stutterer in the management of the problem.

The young stutterer must be encouraged to develop his interests, to express himself through things that he can do well. A special area of his own in which he is improving his knowledge and skill will be something that he can turn to when he feels discouraged about speech failures. Along with being a healthy distraction, it will keep him from spending time feeling sorry for himself and getting into what I have learned to call "mental mischief."

As the stutterer works in his special interest area or on his special skill, he will begin to develop some status in his own mind and in the minds of his peers. As this happens, his stuttering will lose some of its destructive power. Once when I was attending a musical in Hollywood with Dr. Wendell Johnson, Dr. Johnson heard that the orchestra leader, Horace Heidt, was in the audience. After the program ended, we went over to see him, and Dr. Johnson asked Horace Heidt if it were true that he was a stutterer. The orchestra leader replied, "Yes, I had a hard time. I had to get myself established in a role where I had success, and the successful thing turned out to be orchestra work." From small successes, he said, he built up to more major accomplishments, and during that time he apparently got his handicap under control. The rise and fall of the disorder often seem to reflect the rise and fall of psychic pride or confidence in the mind of the individual.

When people have been depressed for some time, they often have trouble thinking of interests that they might develop. This is a place where a counselor can help. In addition to finding and working on projects of particular interest to them, young stutterers should be urged to engage in vigorous exercise regularly—to get outside and walk briskly, to play tennis, to ski, or to swim. Exercise is good for the nervous system, and it is a wonderful aid in combating depression and in getting one's mind off frustrations.

Regular exercise, as well as proper food and sufficient rest, is necessary if the stutterer wants to stay in the best possible physical condition. He should want to do this, not only for the boost it will give his self-respect, but because stuttering, like many other weaknesses, increases when a person's general health declines. Both the confident mood that an individual often enjoys when he feels well and the smooth working of a healthy body are effective in reducing the occurrence of stuttering.

Stutterers should learn to chart their own speech experiences to learn in which situations they are going to be relatively stutter-free. It is important for a stutterer to recognize these bases, so he can say to himself that, although he is pretty bad at one time, he will probably speak well at another. It is also important for him to know that his stuttering is likely to stay concentrated in the places where he usually has trouble and that he need not be apprehensive about its spreading into the places where he has regularly experienced fluency.

In helping him to deal realistically with his handicap, the counselor should help the young person understand that his stuttering is not going to disappear quickly. Hoping, as I did, for a magical, sudden disappearance is a waste of time. But, if the individual understands that much of what seems to be stuttering behavior is his struggle to suppress or hide the primary symptoms of stuttering, consisting of more or less uninvolved repetitions and prolongations, he will see that it is to his benefit not to fight against his blocks. Although I totally disagree with the title of Dr. Martin Schwartz's book, *Stuttering Solved*, I do like his choice of words when he refers to the substantial part of stuttering that is really reaction as ". . . everything you do to avoid getting stuck in your speech, and everything you do to get yourself out of having gotten stuck in your speech." If, for the moment, the young stutterer can accept his stuttering and can relax some of the tension he feels concerning it, the severity of his overt abnormality will decrease. He needs to be helped to develop a temporary tolerance for failure, knowing that in the long run his speech is likely to improve.

The stutterer should be counseled to restrict the extent to which he permits his stuttering to influence his life as a whole. It might be helpful to give him the image of a corner in his life, or of a storeroom, in which he is going to keep his stuttering confined, preventing it from affecting other things that he wants to do.

Often the person's life has become so generally colored by his stuttering that to accomplish this sense of separation he must do some untangling. Stutterers tend to blame everything that goes wrong on their stuttering, and their moods become bound to the state of their speech. It is reasonable to recognize that a discouraged mood can follow a speech failure, just as cheerful feelings can follow a period of fluency. But there are happenings outside the realm of speech that make people feel discouraged or cheerful. A way that a stutterer might begin this sorting out of stuttering reactions from ordinary life feelings is by talking to his normal-speaking friends about their fluctuating moods, to find out what usually makes them feel blue and what gives them joy.

Clearly there will be certain activities that the majority of chronic stutterers will not be able to do, such as being radio announcers, or taking on leadership positions which involve frequent speaking before large groups. But most situations in life are not filled with heavy communication pressures. One's stuttering should not keep him away from a dance or a club meeting, from having a hobby which he shares with other people, or from helping other people in some way. In many of these activities a person's being a stutterer makes very little difference. The stutterer who is trying to keep his stuttering hidden is going to miss having such experiences, and then, later in his life, when he may have made much improvement, he will look back and think what a blasted fool he was.

Every stutterer is cheered when he learns about famous men of the past who were stutterers, such as Moses and Charles Darwin and W. Somerset Maugham. It is also helpful for young stutterers to have models of present-day people who have been able to lead successful lives in spite of their stuttering. For example, Garry Moore, the star of the television program "To Tell the Truth," is a stutterer whose speech is highly fluent. Jack Paar is another excellent example of a celebrity who is a stutterer. His stuttering is sporadic, but it does occur from time to time during his appearances, and, when it does, the casual way he handles it is something that young people might emulate. Once, as I heard him blocking slightly, a woman broke in with a statement of her own. He turned to her with a smile and said, "Please don't interrupt me when I'm stuttering."

Another celebrity who is a stutterer is the country-western star, Mel Tillis. Although he can sing fluently and has won a number of awards, he has difficulty speaking. As he begins to speak, he often announces that he is going to stutter, and then he goes right ahead with an equanimity that is wonderful to see.

■ ── ■

During my own high school years, my obsession with my stuttering was interrupted by World War II. My family, my friends, and I followed the progress of the war closely. I had the much needed feeling of drawing closer to the people around me, that we were all in this together. And, when I listened to the casualty reports, I recognized that there were things far worse than stuttering.

One of the people whose wartime activities I followed closely was King George VI of England. I had been an admirer of his since 1937, when I was twelve. I had tuned in to his first Christmas broadcast that year with considerable excitement, because I had heard that he was a stutterer. Even though pre-recording was beginning to be available in those days, he had chosen to make his speech a live one.

I got the BBC at the right time and heard, through the static, "Ladies and Gentlemen, His Majesty, King George VI." He started without difficulty, but then his speech began to be more and more labored. He paused between words, first briefly, and then the spaces grew longer. I could sense from the rhythms that a block was coming, and I held my breath waiting for it. There was one long silence, brief sounds of vocal struggle, and then quick repetitions out of which burst the word. This happened several times during that early broadcast.

In spite of his impediment, King George continued to speak publicly. He inspired his country when it needed him most. I heard him declare war on Germany in 1939. He was so emotional he could hardly speak, and yet his message was clear. I was thrilled by his love for his people, and I could feel his distress with what they faced.

Although he was never completely free of all traces of stuttering, King George's speech improved enormously during his reign. He was helped by an Australian therapist named Lionel Logue who taught him, among other things, to enunciate the neutral syllable "ah" before a particularly troublesome word. His speeches were carefully pruned so that he wouldn't have to say words that usually caused him to block. In 1951 his final illness began to sap his strength, and he stuttered considerably in his Christmas broadcast of 1951. He died in February of 1952.

I have a portrait of King George VI hanging in my front hall. Over the years my admiration for him has been extended to include all things English. The "Made-in-England" label on a product has special appeal for me. I have enjoyed traveling across the Atlantic on English ships, especially the old *Queen Mary*, to visit King George's country, and when I see the royal ceremonies of Great Britain on television I am always thrilled by their music and traditional pomp.

■ ———————————————————————————————— ■

In November of 1917 my father enlisted in the navy. Twenty-five years later, I tried to do it too. In November of 1942, when I was seventeen, I went down to the San Francisco recruiting office and tried to tell the officers there what I wanted. I stuttered so badly that they sent me into an adjacent room to talk to a psychologist. He said to me, "Say 'Methodist-Episcopal.' "

It was such a strange request that it startled me out of my stuttering. I blurted out "Methodist-Episcopal," and then began stuttering again.

The psychologist sent me back to the first office, where the recruiting officer in charge said, "Well, sign the book so we'll have a record that you were here," and then he sent me home.

Ferryboat, *City of San Rafael*, in 1956 arrives at Martinez, California, on her assigned route of later years.

9

Taking the Offensive

In order to find his real interests, a person must know himself, and he must respect himself. Stutterers have trouble getting in tune with themselves sometimes, not only because they may be depressed, but also because they may be devoting most of their attention to the opinions of other people. Large amounts of energy are expended in bids for social acceptance, while private interests are not given a chance to emerge and to develop.

There is no need for a stutterer to respond to society's whims. He has a right, and a special need, to be selective, to do mainly the things he wants to do. I am grateful to my late aunt, Virginia Murray Palmer, a natural nonconformist, who encouraged me to look outward and to avoid false roles. As I've grown older, I've increasingly been able to follow her advice, to forget my stuttering and to concentrate on finding and pursuing the things in life that really appeal to me.

As I look back, I realize that by the time I had reached my teens I had begun to pursue many of the interests that delight me now. However, during high school and early college, as my preoccupation with my stuttering grew, my involvement in leisure interests such as ferryboats and football faded. How I wish I had known enough to keep those interests alive at that crucial time! They would have been good friends to me and might have kept me from reaching the worst of my phobic states. As Dr. Bluemel once said, "If we could live several successive lives, we might finally learn how to live one correctly."

Later in my life, when I did revive my early interests, they helped me maintain attitudes that worked to improve my speech. Because I feel so strongly that stutterers at an early age should begin to develop interests that will permit them to look away from their stuttering, to lose themselves in a healthy way, I would like to describe the pastimes that have been the most diverting and relaxing for me.

I suppose my oldest and most enduring enthusiasm has been for ferryboats, particularly the old side-wheelers like the ones that used to run in San Francisco Bay, the ones that I watched as a child from my bedroom window. I could tell the time of day according to which boat was on which part of its run. This passion is older than my stuttering; the night before my stuttering began I was happy being on a ferryboat. All my life I have watched ferryboats, ridden those of San Francisco and Puget Sound, boarded others all over the world, taken holidays in places where these boats are running, put paintings of them on my walls. I get a certain strength from them. Occasionally I dream that I see the San Francisco ferryboats running, and I wake up with a momentary joy.

My favorite is the *City of San Rafael*, the last side-wheel ferryboat, which was built for San Francisco Bay in 1924. I have followed her whale-back shape up to the mudbanks of Sausalito, where she's been rotting for more than twenty years, now completely lopsided and about to collapse. Her superstructure must be leaning over at an angle of forty degrees, and an old hermit lives in what is left of her upper deck. On my most recent visit to California I was inside that boat, walking through, putting my feet onto the remains of the paddle wheels. I guess it is a way into my past, almost a part of me.

■ ─── ■

Another interest that began early in my life is football. The first game I saw was in Harvard Stadium on our family trip east in the fall of 1932. Harvard beat Buffalo by more than sixty points. After that, I was a football fan. Perhaps, since I was a rather sickly and not very athletic youngster, I enjoyed empathizing with strength and with a male combat sport.

About three weeks after I started teaching at the University of New Hampshire, a colleague said to me, "Fred, what do you do on your weekends?"

I said, "I go to football games."

Looking at me oddly, he asked, "You have a Ph.D., don't you?"

"Yes," I answered.

"Well," he remarked, "is that a very scholarly way to spend your weekends?"

"I don't care," I replied. "I go there and I shout louder than most of the kids."

Sometimes I think that I have a kind of football family scattered throughout the United States, made up of friends I have acquired through my interest in the sport. One of these is Frank Gifford, the ABC sports announcer who used to play pro-ball for the New York Giants. I have known Frank since we lived in the same dorm at the University of

Southern California in the summer of 1949. He has made a tremendous success of his life; he is nationally well known, but yet he is still the same fine person I first met long ago. Success has not spoiled him.

■ ────────────────────────────────── ■

Throughout my life I have maintained an interest in glass and the many uses to which it can be put. One particular kind, Lalique Crystal, especially the opalescent type, has always been my favorite. My great aunt had a wide assortment of it, and at about the age of eight, I developed a real fondness for it. Lalique, produced in France, is currently very popular in the United States. Especially sought are early pieces of this beautiful glass, those designed by René Lalique, founder of the company near the turn of the century. Marie-Claude Lalique, grand-daughter of René and present head of the company, is delightfully innovative with her newest creations in Lalique, many of which incorporate propitious use of color. I delight in pursuing the literature on this subject and in attempting to obtain various pieces of this crystal from time to time.

■ ────────────────────────────────── ■

When I was a child, I enjoyed our family trips to the east coast, through the Panama Canal, and to Hawaii. As I grew up, I started to travel on my own. It is always stimulating to get away from the old surroundings and the old cues, to discover new ideas and customs, to make new friends, to see some of the many beautiful places for the first time, and to revisit congenial spots.

Most of my favorite landscapes are mountains, or islands, or seas. The sacred mountain of Japan, Fujiyama, and Mt. Rainier, near Seattle, Washington, have thrilled me when I've seen them at dusk or at sunrise.

A moment that I will always remember in my travels came when I was on a ship en route to Australia in December of 1972. We were not far from Tahiti, sailing on a warm night over an absolutely calm sea. There was no wind, and the stars and the moon were reflected in the glassy water. For a long time we seemed to be floating in space without beginning and without end.

I have been back to Honolulu several times since 1935. And I have been twice to Africa, once returning westbound from Australia in 1961, and again in 1973. I am very partial to Capetown with its mountains and sea and numerous ships.

■ ────────────────────────────────── ■

A stutterer must always guard against withdrawing from society because of embarrassment over his affliction. Moving out physically from his home retreat will help him do this, but active relationships with other people will help even more. There is a corrective factor in social relationships that is effective in reducing morbid or unrealistic preoccupations of all kinds.

A stutterer doesn't need to go far to be with people. He can go out to a club meeting in his own school or town, where the fun of sharing common interests is available to anybody willing to turn up. Many of my own most important relationships are with people or organizations within a few miles of my home.

My interest in people has frequently coincided with my love of travel. This might simply be called hero worship. I have not let my stuttering prevent me from taking advantage of opportunities to meet people whose accomplishments I admire. Sometimes these people have been stutterers. At different times in my life I have traveled in order to meet Waldo Coleman, Charles Van Riper, as well as a former governor of Wyoming. On the other hand, some of them have been normal speakers. On my first trip to Majorca I made friends with Temple Fielding, the travel writer, whose books I had enjoyed and depended upon for years.

Once in Granada I met the playwright Thornton Wilder. That friendship continued from its beginning in 1955 until his death in 1975. We got together in the United States and in other parts of the world as well. Once we met in Gibraltar. On another occasion I met him in Edinburgh where a new play of his, *A Place in the Sun*, was going to be presented at the Edinburgh Festival. I went with Albert Schweitzer's party to that play, and then we went to a reception for Thornton, where I was introduced to Nathan Pusey, the President of Harvard. That was a night full of heroes for me!

Thornton Wilder influenced me in important ways. He was a perceptive man, and he saw that I had a problem. Shortly after our first meeting, when I was thirty years old and he was fifty-eight, he said to me, "Fred, I want to give you three bits of advice." That advice summarizes much of what I am trying to say to other stutterers in this chapter. He said firmly and forcefully, "(A) Stop worrying about yourself and your stuttering. You are focusing too much on that. (B) Find some kind of endeavor that you can throw yourself into, that is beyond you, that is creative, and in which you are doing something to help other people, and, above all, (C) Hang onto your sense of humor." This third piece of advice is, in my opinion, the most significant—a sense of humor is the most important trait a person can possess.

Stutterers must not think they can only pursue interests that do not involve much speaking. One of the things I most enjoy doing is speaking Spanish. This has allowed me to enter more fully into the activities of many countries which I have visited, and it has helped me make many Spanish-speaking friends.

I owe much of the pleasure that I have derived from this accomplishment to my brother who encouraged me to begin studying Spanish when I was thirteen years old. After studying the language for seven consecutive years, I thought I would bowl the natives over with my marvelous ability; but, of course, when I first visited Spain, I found that I knew only a little bit—and on what I did know, I stuttered!

After a three-month stay in Majorca in 1955, however, my Spanish improved considerably; and, having been back to Spain many times, I now can speak it well. In the spring of 1973, I was proud to be able to teach a speech pathology course, in Spanish, in Palma.

Most of these interests developed only because I got up my courage and made things happen—went out on the boats and looked up their histories, bought tickets for the football games and went to the stadiums, arranged long and short trips, approached potential friends, and practiced my Spanish with native speakers.

Even though a stutterer knows that the best experiences are ones in which he is making the moves, he will often find himself tempted to postpone the beginning of a project because he is shy or he fears failure. This temptation should be energetically resisted. If the club is meeting tonight, he should go tonight and not wait for the next meeting a week or a month away. If a stutterer wants or needs to know a person who is nearby, he should call him immediately, or go see him personally. If the time and money for a desired trip are available, he should not put it off. My friends tease me about my nonpostponing personality, and I laugh when they do. Sometimes I wonder if they realize how much of my apparently natural aggressiveness is deliberate self-therapy.

I have already referred to the feeling that every stutterer has experienced being on the defensive. In reaching out to follow his own strong interests, a person knows himself to be on the offensive, and, exhilaratingly, to be freely and actively doing what he wants with his life.

As he begins to accumulate areas of expertise, to make assertive choices of things he wants to do, the stutterer will experience surges of optimism about his life in general. A glass of liquid that once would have seemed half empty to him will suddenly seem half full.

10

Stanford

When I graduated from high school, I was accepted to do my college work at Stanford University, in Palo Alto, California. I did not look forward to the seventh of October, 1943, which was the day Stanford's fall semester began. The freshman year is often a difficult one for people who have never lived away from home and have never been totally responsible for themselves. In my case, my fears about stuttering were so extreme that they made the transition doubly hard. In high school the tremors and the phobic panics had for the most part been confined to nuclear situations such as the telephone and recitations, but, as the time to go to Stanford drew near, the anxiety spread so much that I stuttered quite badly even in casual conversation. In fact, I was stuttering in nearly every sentence. My speech was the worst it had ever been, and I could not stop thinking about it.

October 7 came, and my parents drove me down to Palo Alto. Since it was wartime and gas was rationed, they must have saved their coupons for the sixty-six-mile round trip. We arrived on a Sunday afternoon. I was so apprehensive I could hardly walk up the steps of my dorm—a converted fraternity house that in wartime was being used to house thirty freshmen.

In addition to normal freshman jitters and my concern about my speech, I had two additional worries. The first had to do with having to register for the draft on October 8, the day I turned eighteen. Since the previous November, when I had tried unsuccessfully to enlist in the navy, I had lost much of my never-very-abundant confidence, and I wondered what good I could do for my country when I was stuttering my head off this way. "Semaphore corps or smoke signals," I said to myself, as I went down to register. One of the questions on the forms they gave me was "Have you had any college education, and, if so, how much?" I wrote, "One day."

When the recruiting officers realized the extent of my handicap, they classified me 4-F. "Sorry, kid," one of them said to me, "we can't use a soldier who's going to take half an hour to tell us we're sitting on a grenade." My feelings about this rejection were mixed, but I did believe that I had been cut off from an important experience.

My other worry came from my parents' insisting that I enter the Stanford engineering program. They, especially my mother, still felt strongly that an engineering career would be right for me because in it they assumed I would not have to do much speaking. I gave in to their pressuring and enrolled as an engineering major. The normal academic load at Stanford was fifteen quarter hours. I signed up for twelve—five in physics, four in history, and three in math. Even with this comparatively light load, the program, particularly the physics, was too much for me. I took notes in physics class and sat down conscientiously with my homework, but, try as I did to concentrate, my mind kept turning back to my stuttering. I would look down at a page in the physics book and see only a blur.

Based on one hundred, I got a score of twenty-five on the first physics exam, and eighteen on the second. I was so naive I didn't know that I could drop that course if I did it before a certain date. By final exam time I had such a low average in physics there was no point in my bothering to study for the final. I studied for the other two courses instead, and wound up with a C− in history, a D in math, and an F in physics. With 2.0 representing a C average, the minimal level of satisfactory performance, my average was 0.92. A notice stating that I had been put on academic probation was immediately sent to my parents. I am grateful that they did not scold me about it. Even though they never understood much about stuttering, they knew that I was going through a hard time.

■ ───────────────────────────────── ■

My first therapist, Helen, had married a Stanford professor. Early that first fall when she heard I had come to the school, she called my dorm, McKinley Hall, and left a message asking me to call her back. I could not make myself go near the phone to call her. In addition to my usual aversion to the telephone, this situation was a tense one because Helen was someone I admired very much, and I had not seen her in a long time. I knew I would stutter violently and I was ashamed to have her witness my failure. She called again and left a second message. Finally, I got on my bicycle and rode down to her house in Palo Alto to talk to her in person. It was pretty bad—I was very inhibited, substituting words and blocking all the time, but it was far better than it would have been over the phone.

■ ───────────────────────────────── ■

On another occasion, friends of my family asked me to dinner at their home in Palo Alto. As I had done with Helen, I did not use the phone to answer this invitation, but instead I rode into town on my bicycle to respond in person. On the night of the dinner, I sat in dread all through the meal, unable to enjoy the unusual treat of roast beef in wartime, afraid that someone would ask me a question.

Of course, someone did. Where did I go to high school in San Francisco? I went into contortions trying to get out "Lowell." A little later another person asked where I was living on the Stanford campus. I couldn't get the "M" in "McKinley" out, so I said, "Kinley Hall." During the rest of the meal I answered other questions with bits of inaccurate information because I could not say the right words.

■ ———————————————————————————————— ■

A second dinner stands out from my memories of that miserable semester. My mother had the idea of asking everybody in McKinley Hall who wouldn't be going home for Thanksgiving to come up to our house in San Francisco for dinner on that day. Eighteen people accepted. Just before they were expected, I left the house. I simply could not face the prospect of introducing eighteen people to the members of my family. At that time I would have blocked severely on every name. After the guests had all arrived and had introduced themselves, I came home and joined the party.

■ ———————————————————————————————— ■

Early one morning before dawn I woke at McKinley Hall and remembered that I had to telephone someone at eight that morning. I lay there, trying to work my way through the conversation ahead of time, picking out the words, planning various responses to probable questions, getting more and more anxious about the call, until, when it was finally time to get up, I looked back at my bed and saw the silhouette of my body clearly marked in sweat on the bottom sheet.

■ ———————————————————————————————— ■

That was a rough semester. My stuttering was absolutely abominable, and I was under stress almost all the time, trying to study, and losing the battle for decent marks. Over the three months I also lost fifteen pounds. Many of the people in my house, including my roommate, found my stuttering amusing. I did go to a few parties, but I usually was tongue-tied when I had to introduce myself. Once I got so far as saying,

"My name is F-F-F-F-Fred," to a stranger who replied, "May I call you Fred for short?" He was trying to impress two girls who were standing nearby, but, when I laughed, they came over and started talking to me. After a party was underway and there was a good bit of noise in the room, I sometimes could start to relax and find a little fluency.

■ ────────────────────────────────────── ■

When I returned to Stanford for the second semester, I switched my major to Spanish. I had no long-range Spanish-speaking goals—at that time I was only existing from one stuttering crisis to the next, but I knew I could do well in Spanish, and I wanted to remain in school.

To change my major I had to see the chairman of the modern languages department. When he heard me stuttering, he picked up his phone and made an appointment for me with the head of the Stanford speech therapy program, Dr. Virgil Anderson. Dr. Anderson made a recording on an aluminum disc, as I stuttered my way through the story of Arthur the Shirker: "Once there was a young rat named Arthur who could never make up his mind . . .," and then he assigned a student therapist to work with me. My first therapy since elementary school was about to begin.

■ ────────────────────────────────────── ■

During my second semester at Stanford I had many moments of frustration because of my speech. One of these occurred early in the semester when a student from McKinley who had a car offered me a ride to class. We rode down to my classroom building, I opened the door, turned to thank him, and my tongue stuck to the roof of my mouth. I sat there for a minute, looking at my friend and trying to force the words out. Nothing happened. My friend smiled at me sympathetically. Then I got out, banged the car door shut, and walked away, completely disgusted.

But, I was enjoying my new major, college life was becoming easier for me, and I felt supported by the therapy. My speech therapist was a friendly, relaxed person. The therapy program which she was instructed to use with me was for the most part made up of mechanical exercises. We worked on my breathing so that I would learn to take full, diaphragmatic breaths. I read from books, trying to achieve a slow, controlled rate. Part of the program concentrated on relaxation. I would tighten individual parts of my body and then let them go limp. When we first began, she asked me to see how far I could count without stuttering. In January I could not get past "three," but later in the semester I got up to "ten," and in the late spring there was a triumphant moment when I counted to "fifteen" without stuttering.

Stutterers often have trouble with the key words in a sentence. The greater the importance, or what we call the "propositionality," of a word, the more likely it is that stuttering will occur on that word. One morning, in the spring of 1944, I was walking to class when I saw Dr. Anderson walking toward me on the sidewalk. When he was within earshot, he said, "Good morning, Fred. How's your speech?"

I stopped to concentrate on my answer, although the professor kept on walking. "Well, I have im-im-im-im-im . . .," Dr. Anderson, still walking, was now looking back over his shoulder at me. "Improved!" I finally blurted out. He was, by then, half a block away.

But even though I stumbled on the very word I was trying to demonstrate, my speech was improving. My family and my friends commented on it. There was a counter in the Stanford student union where I used to go quite often for breakfast. Early in the second semester, I stuttered badly trying to order orange juice and cereal, but late in the spring a waitress who had been there all year remarked on how much more easily I could not only order my breakfast but could also carry on a casual conversation while I was waiting for it to be served. And I noticed that my phobic symptoms were beginning to weaken.

When phobias begin to retreat, they go slowly, because the stutterer's responses have become deeply conditioned reactions. Suppose that a person who is barefoot has had day after day to enter a room in which the floor is covered with broken glass. Then someone comes in and sweeps up the glass. When the barefoot person next enters, he is prepared for familiar pain, and, although the pain does not occur, he will have to enter that room many more times before he will not automatically adopt the psychological and physical attitudes that he has developed in anticipation of pain. It may be years before that person can enter that room without thinking of pain. Phobic reactions are like this. And the longer the reaction has been in effect, the longer residual memories of it will persist in the mind after the problem has been removed.

Some minor phobic reactions, called *residuals*, will never disappear. Even now, in my fifties, I recognize traces of my early phobias. I'm not upset by them because I consider it natural that these reactions should occasionally surface after having been deeply conditioned for years. Many people have slight phobic reactions to fears that hang over from childhood, and they learn to live with them when they reappear from time to time.

Part of my speech improvement in the spring of 1944 simply reflected greater self-confidence. As had happened in elementary school, having regular therapy made me feel I was no longer alone. The speech clinic therapists said that they had had other stutterers in the program whose speech at the start was as bad as mine, and those stutterers had made significant progress. Calculating the progress that I'd made during the first months of therapy, I extrapolated that I might be cured within a year. My stuttering lost some of its repugnance for me, and, buoyed up by hope, I began reading everything about stuttering that I could get my hands on.

One of the books that I read was *The Stutterer Speaks*, by Conrad Wedberg. In it, Mr. Wedberg tells how he conquered his stuttering with the help of Mabel Farrington Gifford, to whom, along with his wife, he dedicated the book. *The Stutterer Speaks* is also a book of advice for stutterers. Mr. Wedberg states that through self-control, relaxation, and the searching out of childhood traumas, a stutterer could gain control of his speech and become fluent.

The Stutterer Speaks excited me more than any other book I read that spring. In June, knowing that in August I was going to be in Mr. Wedberg's city, Los Angeles, I wrote to ask if I might talk to him.

An appointment was made to meet in the Ambassador Hotel. I was almost nineteen. As I waited for Mr. Wedberg in the hotel lobby, I was filled with nervous excitement. When he came up to me and shook my hand, I thought, "Here at last is the miracle man who is cured of his stuttering." He was about forty-six then. I could detect no hesitation or flaw of any kind in his speech.

We talked about his book and about my stuttering. Later, he told me that at that first meeting I struck him as a severe, helpless stutterer. In spite of my initial improvement following the start of the Stanford therapy, I was still in no condition to handle any strain, and meeting Mr. Wedberg was an important event. I believe I did not get out one single sentence fluently while I was talking to him.

He observed that I was stuttering especially heavily on my "P" sounds. He said that this might have an emotional root—that I might have had a failure in childhood associated with that sound.

I asked him, "What can I do?" He said he thought I needed to share my feelings with someone. He suggested a minister, and he also mentioned Mabel Farrington Gifford.

The next month, September, 1944, I got up my courage, went to the phone, and dialed the number of Mrs. Gifford's San Francisco studio. When she answered, I stuttered severely. She did not even ask my name. I said, "May I see you?"

She answered, "Come at four o'clock."

On my way I told myself that I was about to see the person who had cured Mr. Wedberg. I thought I remembered her vaguely from 1931, but I was startled by her beauty. Very relaxed, she welcomed me and led me into her studio. I was able to appreciate the lovely furniture, the paintings on the walls, the soft colors in the Oriental carpets, as I had not been able to do on my previous visits when I was five years old. She asked me to sit in a wing chair, and she sat down in another. Then she took out a yellow legal pad and began writing down the things I should do.

She told me about her star, which I remembered from my Grant School therapy, and she told me that the first step in gaining control of oneself was to learn how to relax voluntarily. She put me through the progressive body relaxing steps that I had learned in elementary school. I closed my eyes, tensed my feet and let go, tensed my calves and let go, tensed my hips and let go, all the way to the top of my head. With my eyes still shut, I heard Mrs. Gifford say in a soft, convincing way, "Now your whole body is under control. In this complete state of quiet, feel your air flow. The speech tract is perfectly normal without outside interference. It's there as it always has been, there to use with outside interference eliminated.

Mrs. Gifford charged twenty-five dollars for six sessions. As I made out the check, she told me to come back in a week. She said to go through the steps of relaxation every day by myself, and to say over and over in my mind, "I am controlling my whole body."

After I left Mrs. Gifford, I went home to find my parents bursting with curiosity about what I had found. I told them about sitting in the chair with my eyes closed while Mrs. Gifford took me through the stages of relaxation. My father expressed strong displeasure, exclaiming that he believed Mrs. Gifford had used hypnotism.

After I explained that I had already paid for six sessions, my father said, "Well, all right. Go for those six." I didn't argue with him then, but I thought to myself that I would wait and see if Mrs. Gifford could help me. If she were able to do for me what she had done for Mr. Wedberg, nothing would keep me from continuing to see her.

11

Relapse!

So I went back to Stanford for my sophomore year in a very different state of mind from the one in which I had arrived a year before. I had a new roommate, a young man from Montana named David Morledge. The fact that his father was a doctor may have made Dave sensitive to other people's problems. At any rate, he was what Mr. Wedberg had prescribed—a person I could talk to about my stuttering. He seemed to sense when something was wrong, and he was always a support for me. I tried to be the same for him, and I am glad to say that our friendship continued long after we finished college.

I was also in a new dorm, Washington Hall. Along with signing up for classes, I signed up for therapy at the Stanford speech center again, and every week I took the train up to San Francisco for my session with Mrs. Gifford. Having that much help with my speech had a marvelously happy effect. One night I took a girl to the opera. I remember sitting there, not paying much attention to what was going on onstage. Instead, I was going over one of the phrases that Mrs. Gifford had told me to keep in my head: "I am normal, I am normal."

And the fluency was coming. It came extremely fast. I went to the Stanford clinic, but my spirits were mostly elevated by my times with Mrs. Gifford. She was dynamic. She had the power to make the devil himself feel good. She was convinced that the whole thing was psychological, that there was no physical reason for stuttering, and that if my personality were reconstructed my stuttering would disappear.

Her path to personality reconstruction was through the subconscious. She believed that a stutterer's will to speak fluently was overpowered by his subconscious conviction that he could not speak fluently. This conviction controlled the victim's motor centers. The only way to free him was to change his subconscious convictions.

Since Mrs. Gifford thought that the subconscious could most readily be influenced when a person was relaxed, she taught her clients to repeat at bedtime and upon first rising statements about the things they wanted to believe or to accomplish. The statements were also to be repeated during self-imposed periods of deep relaxation during the daytime. This was essentially the art of autosuggestion, which Mrs. Gifford had learned in Nancy, France, from Coué.

The stutterer had to develop self-awareness and control. He had also to acquire a reservoir of positive thoughts, so that in the state of relaxation he would be able to supplant each of his negative convictions with a positive one. Eventually, this constant transmission of positive thoughts would alter the negative nature of his subconscious, and at that deeper level he would believe that he could speak fluently. Clear speech would be the result. Mrs. Gifford cited Mr. Wedberg's recovery as a marvelous example.

One part of Mrs. Gifford's theory which is emphasized in Mr. Wedberg's book, but which did not directly figure in the therapy methods she used with me, was her feeling that stuttering is a symptom of emotional conflict arising from repressed memories of early childhood disturbances. If relaxation and autosuggestion were not effective in eradicating his stuttering, the stutterer would have to search out those early disturbances and determine their link with his handicap. If psychoanalysis was not available or practical, Mrs. Gifford favored the writing of an autobiography as the vehicle for this search.

Mrs. Gifford was convinced that if a stutterer persisted in following her methods he would someday have fluent speech. She believed so sincerely in what she was doing that it almost took on religious dimensions. Although I knew she had once been a severe stutterer, I never once heard her even hesitate in her own slow, calm speech. I wanted to trust her completely.

■ ── ■

Although my speech that fall was the best I could remember, I was still stuttering, enough so that everyone who knew me thought of me as a stutterer. While the phobic reactions were lessening in their terrifying effects, I was still using my old avoidance maneuvers. I had a new excuse for avoiding the telephone—I didn't want to have anything contaminate the tranquility that Mrs. Gifford's thought control sessions had brought to most of my activities.

When the last of the six therapy sessions ended, I signed up for six more. I did not tell my family about it because I did not want to go through the fuss that I was sure my parents would make. I was so desperate to be rid of my stuttering that I think I would have gone almost anywhere, have done almost anything to achieve it. I told myself that Mrs. Gifford was no charlatan, she was the director of the California speech correction program. My mother was holding a thirteen-year-old grudge against one of Mrs. Gifford's assistants. And I was nineteen years old and capable of making decisions for myself.

■ —————————————————————————————— ■

Geraldine, a girl from San Francisco and the daughter of friends of my parents, came as a freshman to Stanford that year. She was one of the young people I knew from home who had always been friendly to me and who never teased me about my stuttering. At Stanford she lived in the building next to mine. I was always glad to see her on the campus. When, occasionally, I took her out to dinner, we compared reactions to Stanford or news from home.

Geraldine had always been rather flighty during her high school years, and soon word got back to San Francisco that she was ignoring her books and was apparently majoring in late night parties with upper-classmen. Near the end of November I received a telephone call from my father who related the gossip about Geraldine and told me that he and my mother wanted me to have nothing more to do with her. Stuttering, I answered that Geraldine was a good friend of mine, but my father was firm. After we hung up, I thought about what I should do. I decided to say nothing to Geraldine about the phone call and to let our friendship continue as before.

On the morning that we were to go home for the 1944 Christmas vacation, I tried to say good morning to my roommate, and all I could get out was "G-G-G-G-G . . ." I was suddenly stuttering more acutely than I had all semester.

Dave looked at me, shocked, and said, "Why, Fred, come on. You don't stutter that badly. Get hold of yourself!" But I couldn't. I kept blocking completely on almost every word I tried to say. I was in a panic because I knew I had been improving so rapidly with Mrs. Gifford. And the therapists at Stanford had spoken about the remarkable way my speech was clearing up. Now, all of a sudden, this devastating inability to talk had reared up without warning!

I packed and took the train up to San Francisco. I had told my parents that my speech was much better. When my father met me at the station and heard my stuttering I saw disappointment on his face. I was humiliated, after boasting about how well I was doing. I had hoped to impress them and to prove to my family the efficacy of Mrs. Gifford's therapy. When we got home, everyone pretended not to notice my regression.

Unknown to my family, I had an appointment with Mrs. Gifford for the next day. I went down to her studio depressed and desperate. What could be causing this terrible relapse? I was counting on her to help me. I went in and tried to tell her what had happened, but I seemed to have no control over my speech at all. She shut her eyes and said, slowly and calmly, "Now, Frederick, we've got to think of con—trol and release, con—trol and release." When I remonstrated, my words were unintelligible. She repeated her phrase several times more, told me I had to do some very serious thinking, handed me a book called *Personality Plus*, and sent me away.

That vacation was two weeks long. I blocked all the way through it. One afternoon I was studying in my room, writing with an ink pen. I accidentally knocked the ink bottle over, and ink spilled over my papers, my book, the fresh blotter, the wood of the desk, and down onto the rug beneath. My mother, sitting in the next room, heard my gasp and called to me asking what had happened. I went to the door of her room, and, as I stood there, trying to answer, I felt as though someone had grabbed me by the shoulders and was shaking me violently. My face, twisted with my struggle to break the tremor, turned red and then purple. I felt as though a gigantic balloon were stretching bigger and bigger, about to burst with a devastating force, and I had no way to protect myself from it. My mother threw up her hands, crying, "Stop it! You're worse than you've ever been!"

Just then the word "ink!" exploded out of me. That was the worst block I have ever experienced. It must have been forty or fifty seconds long. To this day, the word "ink" holds such painful associations that I'm grateful for ballpoint pens.

■ ── ■

After Christmas I had to go to a San Francisco store to exchange a sweater that was the wrong size. As I handed the package to a clerk, I was suddenly stricken with an attack of severe phobic anxiety. The store seemed to be whirling around me, and the clerk's voice asking if he could help me had a strange nasal sound. It sounded as though he were talking through a long tunnel from far away. I saw a spot of light in the distance and stumbled toward it like a drunk. It was the store's front door. My anxiety was so intense that I thought I was going insane.

Outside on the sidewalk, I could feel the buildings around me wavering, as though they were about to tumble down. Our family doctor's office was only two blocks away. I managed to get there and to find him, but I could not tell him what the matter was. All I could produce was a series of meaningless sounds. He gave me a bottle of pills and told me to take one three times a day. Somehow I got home and spent the rest of the day sulking.

A day or two afterward my mother had occasion to ask the doctor to come to see her. From my bedroom I could hear them talking. I listened to hear what he would say about my visit.

"Now, what's wrong with Fred?" he began. "He came down to the office, and he was stuttering so badly I couldn't make out what he was saying. It's got to be something emotional—is he out of money, or in love, or what is it?"

"I'll tell you what's wrong," my mother answered. "One of his old friends from high school is down at Stanford acting up, and we've told him to stay away from her."

I thought, "Oh, gosh, what a blind fool I've been. Of course, that's why I was all upset! And not telling them about going on with Mrs. Gifford probably made it worse. I knew I was coming home, and I expected I'd have to stand up against them!"

■ ─────────────────────────────────── ■

Actually, it was a little more than that. I was beginning to break from my family, to assume responsibility for myself. Going to Mrs. Gifford and seeing Geraldine were momentary symptoms of a larger change. Such change is always difficult for the person who is going through it, because he cannot feel as confident as he must pretend he does. This relapse, which was the most severe I have ever experienced, was my reaction to a conflict of strong feelings within me.

Recognizing the cause of the relapse, however, was not enough to make it immediately disappear. Phobic anxiety and the unusual amount of stuttering continued, diminishing slightly, until Washington's Birthday weekend in late February. Dave and I went down to spend the holiday at Monterey. While we were there, the bad spell ended so suddenly I almost thought I could feel something snap inside me. My spirits lifted abruptly, and my speech was almost back to where it had been the previous fall.

■ ─────────────────────────────────── ■

Later that spring I took a battery of vocational tests offered at Stanford to help me decide what I should do to prepare for a career. I didn't want to find myself in the wrong major again! The tests were long and complicated. The first parts were written, and then I had to see a Dr. Hedges for a concluding oral evaluation.

When I went into his office, Dr. Hedges told me to sit down, and then he started talking. He mentioned three career areas which seemed to suit my interests and abilities, but, by far, teaching seemed to be the best field for me.

He stopped talking and asked me a question. As I answered, a shocked look came over his face and he began to gather up my papers, which were spread out over his desk.

"I didn't know you are a stutterer," he said. "Everything I have suggested to you is invalid. You'll never be able to teach. And you can't hope for the other jobs I described either."

I asked him what he thought I could do.

After a minute, Dr. Hedges answered. "Well, you might be able to work in the post office. But, not at the front window."

I've always had a fuse inside me that, when sparked, can produce fire. Instead of being dashed by Dr. Hedges' words, I was angry. "I will show you! I will, I will!" I said to myself as I hurried out of the building and back to my dorm, determined to squirm out of these verbal handcuffs.

■ —— ■

Many years afterward, on a Sunday night in 1973, I started up the steps of the Harvard Faculty Club in Cambridge, Massachusetts. Sometimes there is no one to answer the door of that building on Sunday nights, but, because I am a member, I had a key. I was getting it out when a man standing below on the walk called up to me.

"What am I supposed to do to get in?" he asked. "I have a reservation for a room tonight, and I'm giving a lecture tomorrow. I'm from Stanford."

"Come on up," I said. "I know Stanford well. I did my undergraduate work there."

As the man came up the steps, the light over the door struck his face and I recognized Dr. Hedges.

My flashback emotions flared up immediately and were startlingly strong. All the outrage that I had felt leaving his office twenty-eight years before hit me again. My temples pounded as I pointed my finger at his face and shouted, "It's *You!*"

The poor fellow stepped back and looked as though he were going to jump over the railing into the bushes, but I controlled myself and tried to explain. "I wanted to prove you wrong," I said, "and I did. I have taught successfully for fifteen years." And then I thanked him for giving me a kick that had made me determined to try harder than ever to improve my speech.

12

"End of the Beginning"

Even though I had discovered what has always seemed to me a major weakness in the Gifford therapy—that it does not allow for the speech failures that are sometimes going to occur when a stutterer is under pressure, I continued to go up to San Francisco for therapy through the 1945 spring semester. And, of course, I went to the Stanford speech clinic as well.

In that spring my two therapy centers came together when Dr. Anderson and Mrs. Gifford were the principal speakers at a speech correction conference held in Palo Alto. I went to hear the lectures, which were given outdoors on a covered terrace with wisteria vines in bloom behind the speakers' platform. I sat there, hoping as usual to hear something that would instantly cure me, never dreaming that one day I would be participating in programs just like this one.

I had reached a point where I was able to speak easily with the Stanford clinician who was assigned to me that semester. As the term neared its end, we learned that Dr. Anderson wanted me to give a little speech before three of his therapists at an informal meeting in June. My therapist and I wrote the speech together, and then we practiced it for several weeks. I could say it without difficulty so long as I was saying it to her.

On the day of the talk, I bicycled down to Dr. Anderson's office, feeling decidedly nervous. The situation was a casual one; the therapists were sitting in easy chairs in a carpeted lounge, and I did not have to stand at a lectern for my brief speech. Nevertheless, I was apparently still unable to speak well under pressure, and I stuttered badly. To my surprise, when I began blocking, my therapist picked up a pad of paper and started to take notes, looking up at me as though she had never seen me before. I suppose she was embarrassed by her student's failure—she was only a student herself. I felt a little down about that incident immediately afterward, but school was ending, vacation was at hand, and I soon became absorbed in a summer plan that involved visiting a friend in Seattle and riding the ferryboats there.

■ ─── ■

The following fall, while my speech was definitely improving, I still had plenty to work on. Mrs. Gifford and I agreed that I should suspend my therapy with her for a while and see how I could get along by myself, but I continued my therapy at Stanford. I had a new therapist assigned to me at the start of the fall semester. The program was pretty much the same rather mechanical one I had been following since I began there. One typical exercise involved my breathing words out at an abnormally slow rate. In another I sang or chanted my words, instead of trying to speak them in an ordinary way. I met the therapist twice a week, and every so often there would be a required group meeting with other stutterers. Instead of hating the subject, I was becoming extremely interested in stuttering. I believed that if the right treatment could be found I could be cured.

■ ─── ■

I still was not able to master my anxieties either about the telephone or about introductions. One beautiful fall afternoon a friend named Bill Baxter and I started out in a borrowed car to drive to the top of Mt. Hamilton to the Lick Observatory, where a girl I had been dating was working. I was in fine spirits when we started, but part way up the nineteen-mile mountain road I suddenly thought that when we got to the top I was going to have to introduce Bill to the girl. Coincidentally, her name was Barbara Branner, and, with my heart pounding, I began to see a big letter "B" hanging in the air in front of me as we came around every turn. And that road is famous for having three hundred sixty-five turns—one for every day in the year! I'm sure you could have used the Palmar Sweat Index to measure the moisture coming out of my hands!

It was late in the afternoon, about time for the sun to set. I silently rehearsed the two names as I drove up the last mile, trying to be ready to get the "B" sound out. As we came around the last curve and started up a five percent incline that runs about four hundred feet straight up to the parking lot at the mountain's summit, there, silhouetted against the sunset sky, was Barbara. I was so startled to see her standing there, and so rattled by the imminent introduction, that I nearly drove straight past her, over the mountain top and down the other side. I did manage to stop the car, however. Barbara said, "Oh, hi, Fred. How are you?" in a casual tone, which must have been a contrast to the way in which I promptly started my struggle with their names. Since then, whenever I've been up at that spot, I've always imagined I saw a little stone marker bearing the single letter "B."

■ ——————————————————————————————————— ■

I was restless, eager to find additional routes to recovery. That December I went down to Los Angeles to see Mr. Wedberg again. During our conversation he told me about a San Francisco man named Waldo Coleman who had been helped by Mrs. Gifford's therapy, beginning in 1913 when he was in his thirties. After his substantial speech improvement, in 1926 Mr. Coleman gave the state of California enough money to start its first state-wide speech correction program. So it was thanks to him that I had the therapy that was a great support for me in elementary school. Mr. Wedberg also told me that Mr. Coleman had formed a San Francisco group for adult stutterers who had been through therapy. The purpose of the group was to share and reinforce the efforts that its members were making on their own to overcome their speech problems.

Mr. Wedberg spoke admiringly of Mr. Coleman and so enthusiastically about the group that I thought I would try to join it. I thought I qualified because I was a college man, and because I had already been in two different adult therapy programs. Although most of the group meetings took place in Mr. Coleman's office at the top of the Russ Building, I learned that the next meeting was going to be held at Mrs. Gifford's studio. When I called her and asked her about my attending, she was not enthusiastic. "Oh, Frederick," she said, "those meetings are for people who already have a good bit of control over their speech."

That slowed me slightly, but I was so wild to get rid of my stuttering that I could not give up any chance for help. On the evening of the next meeting I got dressed up in a suit and arrived at the door of Mrs. Gifford's studio a few minutes after the group was supposed to assemble. When Mrs. Gifford opened the door, she looked surprised. Behind her I could see a number of people standing around talking to each other. I said, "Good evening," and walked in. Mr. Coleman happened to be standing near the door. He looked up, introduced himself, and I came back with one of my bombshell "F-F-F-F-Fred M-M-M-Murray's." Mr. Coleman didn't look at all disturbed. He took me by the elbow and led me into the room. I saw immediately that I was ten to twenty years younger than anybody else in the room.

Mr. Coleman told me that whenever the group met at Mrs. Gifford's studio she would deliver a lecture on one aspect of her therapy, such as the power of the unconscious mind, or the practice of the principles that made up her star. I joined the others to listen to her speak. When she finished, Mr. Coleman invited me to come to the next meeting, which would be held at his office the following week. I didn't look at Mrs. Gifford, who was standing nearby, as I thanked him and said I would be there.

It didn't take me long, at that second meeting, to find out that, not only was I the youngest, but I was by far the worst stutterer in the room. The session began with each person reading a passage from a book that was passed around. After the reading, a group leader launched and directed a discussion of the material that had been read, or a discussion of some timely topic. I later learned that the members took turns being the group leader.

I had an awful time with my reading that night. My words came out at about three per minute. During the discussion I said nothing, but I listened carefully to what each person said and the way he said it. I could see that some of them had been very severe stutterers. No matter how slowly they spoke, it was thrilling to watch the way each one, controlling his breathing and consciously relaxing, got out what he wanted to say.

I went to as many of those meetings as I could. The pressures that I met there intensified my stuttering, and, whenever it became too much for the other members to bear, they would start to give me advice. I was told to relax, to sing the words, to breathe out my sentences, or to speak more slowly. Sometimes at the end of the meetings I had pains in my chest which were caused by my prolonged efforts to speak on residual air. Since my stuttering was so much worse than that of the others, several of the members became impatient and asked Mr. Coleman to expel me. He refused. I was deeply grateful; I was determined to stay with the group because I felt that any improvement I could manage to make in that situation would be a significant advance for me.

Mr. Coleman invited me to visit him outside the group. From the moment I met him I had been impressed by the honesty and kindness in his expression. He became a model for me, not only as a person who had overcome his stuttering handicap, but as an extraordinarily fine human being as well.

■ ── ■

When Mr. Wedberg told me about Mr. Coleman's group, I had never heard of stutterers' voluntarily meeting together for the purposes of mutual improvement and support. Since then, I have met many such groups, and I have always been impressed with the loyalty to the organization that develops in its membership. Because stutterers often retreat socially, those who hear of stuttering groups sometimes say at first that they are not interested, that they prefer not to talk about their problem. But, when this reluctance is overcome, almost every stutterer I know who has visited a group of this kind is convinced of its value.

Adults who are interested in starting a stuttering group, or who would like to learn about possible nearby groups that are already in existence, can write to the American Speech-Language-Hearing Association or to the Stuttering Foundation of America at P.O. Box 11749, Memphis, TN 38111-0749.

■ ———————————————————————————————————— ■

In April of 1946 I read in the Stanford newspaper about a club that was being formed to bring together students and faculty who were interested in travel. I hoped that some interesting ideas for my own, or even for group excursions might come out of it, and so I decided to go. I remember that the first meeting was held after dinner in one of the campus classrooms that held seminars during the day. There were about twenty people there of various ages, all sitting around a big table. One woman seemed to be in charge of the project. She was rather domineering in her manner, and, when the time came, she stood up and said in a positive way, "And now I think it would be nice if we all took the opportunity to. . . ."

Those words. I remember the "I think it would be nice if. . . ." That was all I needed to set off the old standing in front of a firing squad feeling. My adrenalin must have shot to three or four times the normal level in two seconds.

Because I knew very well that she was about to say it would be nice if we stood up, one by one, introduced ourselves, and said where we were from. I didn't think it would be so nice. I suddenly hated these people, and I especially hated that woman who had the audacity to infringe upon my silence. I wanted to escape from the room. The leader of the firing squad was saying, "You can go, you can run away. However, if you don't, I'm going to shoot you dead on the spot." And my body was so weak with fright I couldn't move.

I understand that even normal speakers don't particularly like having to stand up and say who they are. They may get an extra heartbeat or two out of it, but no normal speaker can possibly appreciate what it is to feel this compulsive panic, to feel trapped in this way.

I remember clearly that the woman in charge was to my right as I sat, eight or nine people away from me around the table. The person on her left stood and said his name. All of a sudden my senses began to waver. I could hear the words being pronounced, but they seemed to be coming from a distance, as the speakers changed, one nearer to me and then the next, nearer around the table. Then, it was my turn. I had to stand up and say my name.

I suppose I was set trying to get that "Fred" out at least ten seconds before I had to. But, it didn't come. I felt the way a stuttering friend of mine did in a situation where he said his whole body felt like one big block.

And, I contorted. The faces looked around with various expressions—surprise on some, revulsion on others, pity on still others, mouths gaping open, while I stood there, twisted, wrangling with the demon, gasping, breath inhibited, and the only thing I could do was to let the spasms run their course until I could finally blurt out "Fred."

And then came "Murray." It was even harder, because I was going into tremors. The "M" sound went off in volleys. I felt my body quivering, as though there was no coordination left in any of my parts. All the feeling and struggling. And *then* having to say where I was from!

It seemed like ten minutes. I sat down, and they went on around the table. I don't remember hearing anybody else say his name. Or, what was said during the rest of the meeting. After it was over, I went home seething.

■ ── ■

At that time I had just come across what must have been the first edition of *Speech Correction: Principles and Methods*, by Dr. Charles Van Riper. This book described a whole new way of treating stuttering. It said, in essence, that for the confirmed stutterer the handicap is so embedded that it is impossible to prevent its occurrence altogether. But, it said, a person doesn't have to worry about not being able to stop every bit of it. There are many ways to stutter. It is possible for a person to learn to do it so fluently that he can seem to speak well.

I had gone through several sections of the book, reading about the methods, looking at some of the assignments. Dr. Van Riper said: "Keep a mirror in front of you, put yourself in certain situations, such as using the telephone, where you may stutter badly. Watch yourself, see what happens there. Then go about exploring the possibility of doing something else. Don't try to speak normally, but see if it's possible, through changing the behavior you see in the mirror, the positions of your mouth, to say the troublesome words in a different form of stuttering."

As I continued reading, I began to feel a slight lift. Passages in the book reminded me of my experience at the travel club. I began to put things together. I thought, "Let's see. The second meeting will be two weeks from now." And, I thought, because new people would undoubtedly come the second night, that woman would probably decide to have the self-introductions go all the way around the table again. I said to myself, "If there's a way to at least attempt to change this thing. . . ." So I went and got out a mirror.

I looked in it directly and tried as best I could to make a facsimile of what had happened to me at the meeting. How I loathed what I saw in that mirror—that strained, contorted face, the cheeks and lips pushing! But, as I looked, I somehow understood that this was for me a new and significant kind of self-confrontation.

I experimented to find out what some of the various ways I could change my stuttering might be. Dr. Van Riper wrote about something called a "prolongation" or a "glide." It was possible to make a kind of dragged-out stutter in which the sound could be there without the usual speech mechanism gyrations. Instead of saying "f-f-f-f-five," I could say "f----i----ve." I monkeyed around, looked in the mirror, and thought, "I'm going to try to use this method when that group meets again."

So, I went at it. I began by experimenting with the positioning of my mouth in the way that I said "Fred." Of course, when I was relaxed and alone, looking in that mirror I could say my name normally if I wanted to, without any difficulty. However, the book indicated I shouldn't do that, because when a person is under pressure, normal speech will probably not be one of his choices. But, a person can choose a halfway target, a smoother pattern of stuttering without jaw tremors, that he may be able to carry off effectively.

Looking in the mirror, I practiced over and over again, faithfully, several times a day. Dr. Van Riper stressed the importance of what is called "kinesthetic" or "proprioceptive" feedback—being highly aware of the movement patterns in one's own speech mechanism as the words are being spoken. So I tried to feel the muscles in my face move in different ways—my goal was to reach a point where I would be able to direct them voluntarily.

The sounds I was making might be written out as a slow "F----r--e--d---M---u--r--ray," keeping my jaw loose and the sound moving forward. I began to feel at home with that. It was as though I could go right into that behavior by lightly pressing a button in my body. I felt as though I were fortifying myself.

The night of the meeting arrived. Many of the same people were there, but there were a few new faces as well, and, sure enough, my prediction came true. That same woman, sitting in the same seat, started out with the same words, "I think it would be nice if . . . ," and I was hit by the same emotional flood, my heart going to my feet, my breath getting short, all the familiar reactions.

However, there was a difference this time. There was a voice in me that said "Murray, now come on. You've only got one job to do. Let the emotions occur, but you have to see if you can steer this mechanism." The feeling of a gun about to go off was in the room again, but, for the first time, I was not totally its helpless victim. The gun was in my hand and, partly at least, under my control. If, holding the gun steady, I could voluntarily pull the trigger very slowly, the firing wouldn't hurt me.

They started in. As I remember, I was again eight or nine seats away from the first speaker. I thought of only one thing. I focused on that mechanism inside my mouth, keeping my face relaxed, just visualizing myself in my mirror, and, when my turn came, I stood up slowly, deliberately, and said, "Fred Murray from Washington Hall," exactly the way I had practiced it at home.

Nobody batted an eye. I'm sure there were those who remembered me from two weeks before and had said to themselves, "Oh boy, here he comes again, that poor fellow." But, I fooled them.

And, I partially fooled myself. I thought that was the beginning of the end. The end has never come. To borrow from Winston Churchill, this *was* the end of the beginning. For me, it was a turning point, the beginning of effective control. Dr. Van Riper was right when he said that what the stutterer needs to be on the way to major improvement is just a few key events where he's been swept down the river before, and where, for once, he's going to hold onto something and not get swept away.

To this day I still feel a thrill when I remember that night, so many years ago.

The author in Monterey Peninsula about 1948.

13

Quest

Every person who has begun life without a handicap and then developed one knows that many yearning thoughts go back to the time when nothing was wrong, when "I was normal." Near the end of May, 1946, I decided to act on an idea that had been in the back of my mind a long time. If I returned to Yosemite, I might find the part of me that was missing, that was keeping me defective. Several romantic notions were involved. I remember hoping that if the search were conducted in as honest a manner as possible I might be rewarded with the answer I desired. I knew that long ago in Yosemite I had been a normal speaker. What I was undertaking was a quest to find my normal voice.

Today it seems naive to me, but then I was young and desperate. Just before Memorial Day weekend I went up to San Francisco, talked my mother into lending me her 1937 Plymouth, and started out.

To go to Yosemite National Park from the coast entails crossing a great valley, the San Joaquin, which is flat. To the east can be seen foothills and, behind them, mountains. It was a warm day, the sky was blue, and when I first looked ahead and saw the mountains in the hazy distance, I told myself that I was heading back into a world that I had left years ago. In those mountains there was a treasure for me to find.

However, as I drove nearer, I told myself that this was a wild goose chase. My foolish heart was arguing against my common sense, and with every mile I grew more distressed.

I knew that in 1928 we had stayed at Yosemite Lodge. It was in one of the tents there that I had had my severe nosebleed. So I went directly to Yosemite Lodge. To my disappointment I was told that they had no space available. The man behind the desk suggested I try Camp Curry, a short distance away. I did this, and found a place there, but already the perfection of the quest had been slightly marred.

I was shown to my quarters, a Camp Curry tent that had a wooden foundation, and, as soon as I was alone, I lay down on the bed and looked up at the tent's canvas roof. I tried to concentrate back to the child I had been in June of 1928. "I go back, I go back," I said over and over, trying with my will to reconnect the wires that had short-circuited in this valley. Outside the tent's screen the sun was shining through the surrounding trees. I could hear birds chirping, and faintly in the distance I could hear water rushing over rocks. Nature was showing me beauty, but she was telling me nothing.

After awhile, I got up and went outside. I felt impelled to get physically above this place, so I asked directions and started driving up to Glacier Point. After following backroads up through woods that grew on a steep slope, I drove out onto a great bare cliff. It was a magnificent spot. I left the car and walked to the cliff's edge. Camp Curry and Yosemite Lodge were three thousand feet below me. At the bottom of this granite wall, there in that valley, I had once been able to talk without stuttering.

Irrational or not, I did have a brief surge of hope as I stood on Glacier Point. The late spring sun was warming the granite. I sat down and took comfort from the heat that I felt radiating from the rock's rough surface. Even though summer was near, I could see snow patches in the crooks and hollows of the high mountains, above the evergreen stubble on their slopes. Yosemite Falls hissed faintly in the distance. A gust of down-valley breeze splayed the mist of the upper falls so that for a moment there was a rainbow. "Maybe that's a sign," I thought.

But then clouds moved across the sun, and the air turned cool. The stone beneath me began to lose its heat. Still nothing had happened. I looked at my watch and saw that the afternoon was over. Dinner was already being served in the Camp Curry dining room below. There seemed to be no point in staying longer on the cliff, so I got up and started back to the car.

Down on the valley floor the gigantic landscape seemed suddenly threatening. The peaks leaned slightly inward over the valley, looking as if they could, if they wanted to, curl inward from both sides like two fists. I felt miniaturized and enclosed. And I felt ridiculous. I had recognized nothing. I was crazy to have made this trip at all. In the dining room I stuttered badly to the waiter as I tried to order my dinner. I wanted to throw the menu on the floor.

After dinner when it was dark, I watched the famous Yosemite firefall. A fire is built at the brink of the Glacier Point precipice. When its embers begin to glow, they are pushed over the edge of the cliff, making a spectacular fireworks display. A traditional Indian chant is called out as the sparks are falling. On a still night it can be heard in most parts of the valley. I heard it, and it said to me: "Toss away this silly idea as those embers are being tossed over the edge of the cliff. There is nothing for you to find here."

Early the next morning I paid my bill and started back to Stanford. While the trip did exorcise my fairy tale dream of finding clear speech in

Yosemite, the experience was a deeply depressing one for me. Its effect lasted for some time.

On the day following my return I decided to take advantage of my borrowed car and to ride around the Stanford campus. I had promised my mother I would return her car on Monday. As I was going through one intersection, the sun was in my eyes. A car came suddenly from the right and hit my back fender. My car spun end to end two or three times, then tipped into a ditch beside the road. The other car stayed on the road, but its front was bashed in and water was leaking out of its radiator.

No one was badly injured. A woman in the other car had a slightly scratched leg, but I think she was more upset about a run in her nylon stockings, which were extremely hard to find then, just after the war. I had a tiny scratch on my forehead out of which only one little drop of blood came, but that made me legally bleeding, so when the police arrived, they took me to the Palo Alto hospital for a physical examination.

My more substantial injury was emotional. I was momentarily in shock, and, although immediately after the accident I got out of the car and climbed up onto the road, for at least five minutes I could not make a single sound. The people in the other car spoke to me and made me sit with them while we waited for help to come. When I was finally able to speak, I stuttered severely.

And then, very early on Monday morning, I had to take the train up to San Francisco, face my mother, who was still in bed when I arrived, and tell her that I had done $240 worth of damage to her car. I'm glad I don't have to live through those four days again!

■ ───────────────────────────────── ■

In 1946 the speech therapists at Stanford began to add psychological techniques to the mechanical suppression techniques that they had been using with stutterers. One of the innovations was psychodrama, in which the stutterers acted out various roles that the therapists thought they needed to be exposed to. The theory behind role playing was that the stutterers would gradually overcome their phobias if they were forced, in play, to confront fearful situations. For instance, I might introduce two people in a psychodrama, or I might pretend to be talking over the telephone. Once I pretended to be a dissatisfied customer taking a loaf of stale bread back to a bakery. My speech was fluent in the psychodramas, but I noticed no improvement when I tried to speak in Mr. Coleman's adult stutterers' group.

Our psychodrama therapy went on the road when the therapists decided to put together a psychodrama program and perform it for speech correction groups at nearby colleges. One night we put on a show at San

Francisco State College for a large audience. The program was recorded. Ordinarily, either the audience or the recording machine would have sent most of us into stuttering convulsions. But, as long as we were pretending to be people other than our real selves, we got along fine.

The young man who was my therapist at that time added other psychological techniques such as the Rorschach or inkblot test to my therapy, but his chief interest was in working with rate control. This is a therapy procedure in which the stutterer speaks slowly and evenly in time to a metronome or some other timing device. It worked for me in that it temporarily stopped my stuttering, but, of course, my speech was hardly normal in its sound.

The mechanical therapy, the psychodramas, and the rate control devices were all momentarily successful because they were employed in an artificial atmosphere that was protective and supportive. In a speech on finding truths about stuttering, Dr. West once said that the laboratories and clinics in which many stuttering theories have been developed are like the tops of mountains where the air is so thin that minds tend to become deluded. An avid mountain climber himself, he said that people who climb mountains and reach the heights often think they are looking directly into the face of truth. From the tops of many mountains have come what seem to be important discoveries about stuttering, but, said Dr. West, whatever the facts seem to be on top of the mountain, they can't be trusted until they are tested down in the valley of the real world.

I found out how hard it was to transfer my clinic fluency into the real world when, in the fall of 1946, I signed up for a course that entailed public speaking. I was trying to prove to myself that I could overcome my handicap in a pressured situation, but I failed. I can recall very few speeches in that class that I handled well at all, and it got to the point where I felt sorry for the other students because of the strain my stuttering put on them.

At the end of the semester the professor told me that I had a good loud voice, I had good modulation, clear emotion—especially enthusiasm, and, if it were not for my stuttering, he said, I could be a good speaker. I didn't know whether to be depressed or to be cheered by that evaluation.

I had to face the truth that, while under normal circumstances my speech was now generally good, whenever stress appeared in real life I had found no efficient way to deal with my stuttering. The only exception was my one elaborately planned success with five words at the travel club meeting. I had a terrible feeling that once I began to stutter there was no chance of my getting my speech under control, and I was afraid that no one who heard me in that condition would ever hire me.

■ ─── ■

By February of 1947 I had been going to the adult stutterers' group for fourteen months. Almost every Monday I had taken the train up to San Francisco to meet with Mr. Coleman and the others, and every time I went there I stuttered violently. In no other situation has my stuttering been so continuous from arrival to departure; every time I opened my mouth there was a battle. And over all those months I could see no change.

I suppose my being much younger than the other members created part of the pressure that I felt—several of them were in their sixties. Most of them were successful in their careers, while I was just a college student who didn't even know what he was going to do after graduation. But the major difference between the other members and me was that they could control most of their stuttering, while in their presence I seemed to lose every vestige of control. My feelings of panic were so overwhelming that I could not possibly use Dr. Van Riper's prolongation technique. I could not calm down enough to think how to do it. I knew Mrs. Gifford had been right when she said the group was beyond me.

And yet I could not stop going. It was not because anyone there had challenged me. I could not reason out my behavior then, and I cannot totally understand it now. Although attending was torture, it was valuable. Perhaps being with many adults, all of whom had known firsthand what I was going through and who had triumphed over this chaos, inspired me. Perhaps it comforted me. Perhaps my old wishes for magic were operating, and I thought I could catch the others' fluency simply by being near them. Whatever the reason, I needed to be with those people every Monday night, even though humiliation was virtually guaranteed.

And then one Monday noon in February I knew that the struggle was over. My speech the preceding week had been no better, and nothing unusual had happened. I had no reason for expecting a change, except that there had been a shift in the way I felt inside. I went to the meeting, and it was true. When Mr. Coleman asked me to comment on something that had just been read, my speech was ninety-seven percent better than it had ever been before in that room, and in subsequent meetings it stayed that way. The members could hardly believe I was Fred Murray.

Explanations can always be hypothesized for unanticipated reversals of this kind. I may have worn out my panic. Or, from familiarity, my fears may finally have subsided to the point where I could apply Dr. Van Riper's technique—even far enough so I could find the fluency I was achieving in ordinary casual conversations. The improvement may have been growing unseen for some time; in many endeavors progress will come in a sudden spurt after a long period in which nothing has seemed to change. I must have held some hope all along that I could fight my way through my inhibitions, my sense of inferiority.

The most significant aspect of the entire experience was one which I did not appreciate at the time. This was that for once I had hit a pressure area and not retreated. I had not avoided or tried to hide my stuttering: Without shame I had plunged blindly ahead, trying to fight my way through the problem to its solution.

■ ── ■

After I first read the name of Dr. Van Riper in his book, I began to hear it in the conversations of the Stanford therapists, some of whom talked about hearing him speak at national speech convention meetings. Although he had once been a severe stutterer, they said they had not heard him stutter at all. I also began to hear the name of Dr. Wendell Johnson, another stutterer who had become a specialist in his own affliction. The therapists told me that Dr. Johnson was having unusual success in his work with stutterers at The University of Iowa.

As soon as I heard that, I headed for the library to find out more about the Iowa program. In some ways the therapeutic outlook at Iowa was similar to the one I had discovered in Dr. Van Riper's book. The Iowa therapists were not trying to eliminate stuttering altogether—they were trying to teach people how to stutter more fluently. Instead of building systems for suppressing stuttering, they were helping their patients to reduce avoidance maneuvers and to accept themselves as stutterers. The therapy involved the use of both mechanical and psychological techniques. I was so impressed with what I read and heard about the Iowa clinic that I wrote to Dr. Johnson and was accepted to attend the clinic's 1947 eight-week summer session.

14

Off to Iowa

I started out for Iowa on a small DC-3 airplane that, like all commercial flights of the time, was scheduled to make many stops along the way. As my father saw me off from the San Francisco airport, my mother tuned in at home to the radio news and heard that the worst storm in fifty years was approaching the Rocky Mountains. We stopped first at Reno, then went on to Salt Lake City, where the storm delayed us for more than an hour. We did fly on to Denver, but then I had to take a train from Denver through Nebraska and into badly flooded sections of Iowa. When I finally got to Iowa City, I was a whole day late.

It was exciting to be about to enter a speech clinic that was famous, not only for the work that was currently being done there, but for historical reasons as well. From my reading I knew that it was primarily at The University of Iowa that Drs. Lee Edward Travis and Samuel T. Orton had developed their theory that stuttering results from the lack of clear-cut dominance by one side of the brain (referred to in Chapter 2), and it was to this clinic that Drs. Wendell Johnson and Charles Van Riper had come for help in 1926 and 1931.

I found the clinic in the basement of East Hall, formerly a hospital, and went into the administrative office to enroll. While I was standing there talking to the secretary, I heard someone stuttering in the hallway. I thought, "Here comes someone who is also enrolling." Then the door opened and in came Dr. Wendell Johnson.

By that time I knew much about him, having read his 1930 book *Because I Stutter*, which portrays better than any other book I've read what it is like to be a stutterer. And I had read the book he'd published in 1946, *People in Quandaries*. I had seen several pictures of him, and I knew that he had received the Honors of ASHA, its highest award.

But, still, it was a disheartening shock to discover that the man under whom I hoped to learn how to eradicate my stuttering was actually in some ways more of a stutterer than I was. Since then I have learned that there are many ways to look at stuttering, and there are many degrees of improvement. Because someone stutters noticeably does not mean that he may not have made as much progress as others who do not seem to stutter as much.

I was assigned to a therapy group of fifteen stutterers, fourteen men and one woman. Two or three of them hardly stuttered at all. Partly because I was avoiding situations where I thought I would have difficulty, my speech sounded better than most. A few were extremely severe—I remember an instance in which one fellow stayed stuck on a single syllable for three minutes and twenty seconds.

The director of the stuttering therapy and my clinician at Iowa was Joseph Sheehan, who was then twenty-nine years old. He had been a bad stutterer himself before he found his first relief at Dr. Van Riper's clinic in Michigan. By 1947 Joseph Sheehan's speech had greatly improved. His stuttering was very mild, similar to what we call "cluttering"—a choppy, broken kind of speech that is characterized by occasional hesitations, revisions, and repetitions—but he was not really blocking, and he had a very good flow. Since 1947 his speech has cleared to the point where today his is one of the most outstanding improvements I have known. He seems to be able to speak well in any situation. He has become a national authority on stuttering and has been on the faculty at UCLA for more than thirty years. Many of his observations and suggestions about stuttering have been extraordinarily helpful to me, both in my own improvement and in my work with others.

▪ ────────────────────────────────── ▪

There was a marvelous *esprit d'corps* in that Iowa therapy group. Besides having individual therapy which concentrated on each person's specific needs, we met as a group every day for two hours of lecture, discussion, and verbal experiences. Our lecturer was usually Joseph Sheehan. In one of his earliest talks he said that nobody speaks perfectly, that even normal speakers will stutter a little at times. Many of us were so involved in our own struggles that we had never appreciated this. It made us feel less conspicuous and strange. In another of his lectures he reminded us that we didn't have to be cured to achieve success, that many people were leading productive lives in spite of their stuttering.

In group discussions, such as the discussion in which we shared our most embarrassing moments involving stuttering, we released a good many emotions. In addition, we prepared speeches to deliver before the other members of the group.

Almost everything we did was designed to make us relinquish our avoidance maneuvers and accept ourselves as stutterers. If we could accomplish this, we would be liberated from a tension that had gripped us for most of our lives—the strain of trying constantly to hide or suppress our stuttering. To this end, the Iowa pathologists had made up a number of individual and group activities or assignments that, depending on our special vulnerabilities, struck us as useful, amusing, devilish, or brutal.

One of the things we were forced to do to reduce our avoidances was to make ourselves talk more, especially in feared situations. We were required to seek out at least one feared situation every day, go into it, and then write a description of the experience. We listed our successes and our failures, including as failures word substitution, the use of a starter sound to get into a word, the use of unnecessary body movements while speaking, the use of any crutch that interfered with natural fluency, and the dodging of any speaking situation.

More difficult, and sometimes even bizarre, were the activities invented to make us accept ourselves as stutterers. Because stutterers often look away from their listeners when they are stuttering, thereby losing contact with the listeners and increasing their own feelings of being ashamed, one of our assignments was to write down the color of ten persons' eyes after we had stuttered while speaking to them, and another was to write down twenty-five words we had stuttered on without losing eye contact with our listeners.

We stopped strangers on the Iowa City streets to ask directions, putting fake stuttering into our speech as we did so, to have the conscious experience of saying clearly to the outside world that we were stutterers.

For one assignment I had to open the door of an Iowa City shop and ask the people inside: "Is Fred Murray there?" After I was sure I had everyone in the shop looking at me, I would shout: "He stutters!" For another assignment I was told to go into town and, stuttering, apply for jobs in four different stores.

Although I wanted to take advantage of the opportunities for improvement that all the assignments offered, there were so many of them, and some of them were so painful, that occasionally I carried out one in a rather hasty way. I think I filled that job application requirement by tearing through town, dashing into four supermarkets and whipping out a quick "Oh, s-s-s-s-sir, do you have any good jobs here?" to each store manager, who, to my relief, said no. Each one took about fifteen seconds, and I'm sure that's not the kind of job interview that the Iowa clinic people had in mind.

I was also supposed to have the experience of reading aloud five or six times a day to someone, beginning each reading session by saying "Listen to this." I had always detested reading aloud, so I was glad when I found a man of ninety who was deaf and whose mind was rather cloudy living in the boarding house next door to mine. Every day I would go over, take a newspaper, and sit down in a chair near the spot where he sat rocking and smoking cigarettes. I would open the newspaper, say "Listen to this" to my friend who, between his deafness and his dazed mind, hardly knew I was there, and then I would read a few lines. "Listen to this" I'd say again to the rocking cloud of cigarette smoke, and then go on and read a paragraph from another article. Because I did it eight or ten times, I half convinced myself I was meeting, or even overdoing, that assignment, and then I would rush on to another exercise.

We were taught many ways to reduce our anxieties about speaking, which, of course, resulted in our stuttering less. One suggestion was to maintain what Joseph Sheehan called a "safety margin" in our speech. Instead of continually straining for perfect speech, a person could keep his listener from knowing how good his speech could really be by putting in some voluntary stuttering. In this way he could oversatisfy his fears about stuttering and could have the security of knowing he was able to speak more fluently any time he wanted to.

Our mechanical therapy consisted for the most part of learning two speech patterns which would help us gain control over our stuttering. The first was the prolongation or slide, the pattern I had discovered in Dr. Van Riper's *Speech Correction: Principles and Methods*, and used successfully at the Stanford travel club meeting. With the prolongation we could voluntarily hold onto the initial sound of most words until we were able to move ahead to the next sound. If, using the prolongation, I were to say an old nursery rhyme, it might come out as "M----ary had a l-----ittle lamb."

The other speech pattern was new to me. It was called the "bounce." This is the voluntary repetition of the initial syllable of words. The bounce was developed by Iowa speech pathologists with the idea that stuttering is involuntary behavior which takes place in the subcortical part of the brain, and that, when stuttering is occurring, the cortex, or higher part of the brain, is not very effective in monitoring, or controlling, speech behavior. The theory behind bouncing is that, using the bounce, the stutterer can turn involuntary, subcortically instigated behavior into behavior that is voluntary, or cortically controlled. In˙ the process the strain on the speech mechanism and the general struggle behaviors that are so evident during heightened stuttering are dramatically reduced. Instead of wild choking when I try to say my name, how much better it is if, with control, I can say, "Ma-Ma-Ma-Ma-Ma-My na-na-na-name i-i-is Fr-Fr-Fr-Fr-Fred!"

Sometimes, using the bounce, a stutterer will fight his way into control of a block that is already underway. With both the prolongation and the bounce he can begin to feel, as I did in my travel club experience, that he is gaining mastery over something that has been completely dominating him, that at last he has a chance to direct the shape of his own speech.

When we were first taught to bounce, the clinicians told us to be sure to vary the number of bounces that we used on different words to avoid creating a habitual pattern of syllable repetition. This is an important caution for a stutterer to keep in mind. Many times a stutterer will mean to vary his bouncing, but then he will forget and a pattern will form. There is also some danger with bouncing, of creating a dependency situation in which the stutterer reaches a point where he overuses the bounce. This danger is slight because, in my experience, very few stutterers are willing to use it much when they are not in a clinic because they say it sounds ridiculous, even worse than their stuttering.

Dr. Johnson was willing to use the bounce in the outside world. That is what I had heard him doing as I was enrolling. When I first knew him, he did a tremendous amount of bouncing. Later, as his speech improved, he bounced less, and by the time he was fifty, he was speaking very well indeed. Some stutterers, who are recognized professionals in the field of speech today, still use bouncing occasionally, even though their speech is essentially very fluent.

■ ─── ■

As far back as 1931, when Dr. Van Riper went to the Iowa clinic to have therapy under Dr. Travis and Dr. Bryngelson, an important part of the Iowa program was the encouragement of voluntary stuttering. Voluntary stuttering in those days meant more vigorous pseudo-stuttering than simply the bounce or the prolongation. This, modified, was the fake stuttering that we used downtown in Iowa City as we carried out assignments that were meant to make us accept ourselves as stutterers. Dr. Bryngelson believed strongly in the psychological benefits of voluntary stuttering, maintaining that it fostered realistic attitudes toward the handicap, that it enabled stutterers to discard their avoidance crutches, that it reduced fear of stuttering, that it led to the development of confident attitudes, and that it reduced hypersensitivity.

The nonpsychological value of frequent voluntary stuttering, according to Dr. Bryngelson, was that it exercised the higher voluntary or cortical centers of the brain, encouraging cortical or voluntary dominance of the speech function and reducing the amount of speech incoordination that was assumed to be occurring on the subcortical or involuntary level. Along with this mobilizing of speech energy on the highest levels of the nervous system, the therapy was also believed to conserve much of the nervous energy that in uncontrolled stuttering is dissipated at the lower levels.

The assignment of voluntary stuttering was not confined to our activities outside the clinic. At dinner time we were required to stutter voluntarily while speaking about the food. We were also required to stutter voluntarily on the first nonfeared word that we spoke to the first person we met each day.

Every so often ASHA arranges to have what it calls a "Recovered" Stutterers' Panel at one of its national meetings. (Most pathologists believe that a complete recovery from advanced stuttering is impossible.) On these panels, stutterers whose speech has significantly improved talk about the attitudes, therapy, or events that have mattered most in their improvement. I spoke on the panel which was held in November of 1977.

On the 1968 "Recovered" Stutterers' Panel, speaking about the prolongation, one panel member said, "The desirable thing about having an established pattern of stuttering is that you know how you're going to stutter. If a long prolongation is the worst thing that can happen to you, it will not be a true disaster."

On the same panel, another speaker seemed to sum up in a few words the sense of psychological triumph that a stutterer feels when he moves from defensive involuntary stuttering to the offensive voluntary kind. He said, "I'm willing to do the thing I fear."

At Iowa that summer, in addition to individual and group therapy work, I took a University of Iowa course in speech pathology which was taught by Dr. Johnson. It was a difficult course with difficult examinations. Seventy-five students registered for that class, which was held in a room that had been a laboratory. There were Bunsen burners and other fixed equipment on a counter in the front of the room. Dr. Johnson used to come in, hoist his large frame up onto the counter, and lecture. He was a heavy smoker then, and during class, he smoked continually. He seemed to be very relaxed during his lectures. He made me think of a big, lovable shaggy dog, sitting up there with his feet draped over the side of the laboratory counter.

For a person as conditioned to avoidance as I was, it was amazing to watch the free way this man would go ahead and let himself stutter. He stuttered several times per minute, doing a lot of bouncing, particularly on words that began with "s," or with an "s" blend such as "st" or "sp." I could see him approaching trouble, with a slowing down in his sentence speed. He would begin to be geared for it, there would often come a quick eye closure, and then he would, ". . . at the," a pause, "at the sp-sp-sp-speech clinic." Usually he would bounce three or four times, varying the number in accord with his therapy teaching, but sometimes he went higher. Once I counted fifteen bounces before he said the word.

After my disheartened reaction to his stuttering on my first day in Iowa, I soon switched around and began to sense the depths of Dr. Johnson's character and intelligence. Instead of feeling let down because he was still stuttering, I learned to marvel that he had advanced as far as he had up to that time.

I enjoyed his lectures very much. In an early one he talked to us about an imaginary boy named Henry. Dr. Johnson wrote on the chalkboard a list of all the factors that contributed to Henry's being a stutterer. He said that he did not know how Henry could get away from every one of these problems, but he said that he did know it was possible to get over much of the fear of stuttering. He said that all the people enrolled in the clinic program were really there for just one reason, and that was to get over the fear.

He told us how he had improved his own speech through a semantic reorientation, by learning to use a problem-solving kind of language in which he talked about what he did to interfere with his speaking. He said, "Stuttering is not something that happens to me. It is something that I do."

He told us about his 1940 meeting with Alfred Korzybski. From Korzybski, Dr. Johnson learned about the process of symbolization—how we decipher our experience and express it to ourselves. He began to question himself as to what he meant when he said he was a stutterer, and in the process he began to appreciate the importance of the language that he used to describe himself to himself. He said he discovered that the kind of language he used could influence his behavior, and it was at this point in his reasoning that he decided he had to develop a problem-solving language. For instance, instead of saying he was a stutterer, he preferred to describe what he was doing that interfered with his talking. "I held my breath. I tensed my lips."

In order to develop the problem-solving language, Dr. Johnson said that he had to learn precisely what it was he was doing to interfere with his talking; and, once he had discovered what those interferences were, he had to learn what the possibilities were of doing something else in their places. In the process of making these discoveries, he did a great deal of talking, which he said further helped his speech to improve.

Finally, Dr. Johnson reached a point where he believed that much of stuttering results from a person's efforts to avoid it. I know that a great part of my own stuttering has been made up of things I have done to avoid stuttering.

But I have not been able to go as far as Dr. Johnson did when he decided that stuttering arises primarily from faulty perception. He said that stutterers have been trained by society to become conscious of the repetitions and prolongations which occur naturally in the speech of small children. The concept and the label of stuttering are created, he believed, in the ears and minds of the listeners.

Beyond our professional relationship, Dr. Johnson and I developed a friendship. Several times that summer he invited some of the stutterers from the clinic to visit him at his home, which was on the opposite side of the Iowa River from the university campus. We met Mrs. Johnson, their son Nicholas who was then twelve, and their daughter Katy Lou who was eight. I saw him on and off throughout the years, and we kept up a correspondence until he died in 1965. The letters which he wrote me while I was in the service were especially precious, because, in addition to friendly support, they provided intellectual stimulation in the field that interested us both.

In 1947, however, I was only beginning to think I might like to enter the field of speech pathology. I went to ask Dr. Johnson's advice on the subject. He was not encouraging. He told me about many stutterers he knew who had attempted to enter the field and had failed. He said, "You can see I've made it. I'm director of this clinic. But even though I have improved my speech more than ninety percent over what it was ten or fifteen years ago, being in this profession can present special problems. Can't you find another career where your chances of success will be greater?" This candor and openness about himself were typical of Wendell Johnson.

■ ——————————————————————————————— ■

At least once every day that summer I heard the name of Charles Van Riper, especially from Joseph Sheehan who had been one of his early cases. At Iowa I was encountering again some of the ideas that I had first found in Dr. Van Riper's book, and I knew I owed to him my first experience of speech control under pressure. I got the idea that I would like to meet him and to thank him in person, so I gathered up my courage and telephoned him in Kalamazoo, Michigan, to say I had read his book and had heard about him from Joseph Sheehan. Could I take the train to Kalamazoo and meet him? I stuttered like everything, but I got it out, and he said to come.

I went to Kalamazoo with another stutterer from the Iowa therapy group. Dr. Van Riper met us at his clinic. He was dressed in casual clothes, he spoke to us in a very relaxed way, and he made us feel so comfortable that my speech was pretty good while we were talking to him. It was fascinating to meet this man. We talked about our program in Iowa and about what Dr. Van Riper did with his stutterers in Michigan. The programs were similar in many ways: The main difference between Dr. Johnson's and Dr. Van Riper's therapy methods at that time was that Dr. Johnson would rather a patient go ahead and stutter in a relaxed way, using some bouncing, not trying very hard to control his speech, his aim being to reduce the stutterer's fear and to encourage him to speak, maintaining a forward flow; whereas Dr. Van Riper put more emphasis on teaching his patients to work at controlling their stuttering, often using the prolongation technique.

On that first visit with Dr. Van Riper I thought his speech was faultless, that he was cured forever of stuttering. Later I observed that sometimes he allowed himself to stutter freely and fluently in certain situations. Because he has mastered control techniques, he has the ability to change the way his speech sounds at any moment, to make it as fluent as is necessary for the situation in which he is speaking.

■ ── ■

During my last week at the Iowa clinic, Joseph Sheehan told us that there was going to be a radio broadcast in which most of the stutterers were to participate. Immediately I had to know if it were going to be ad lib or if we were going to read from a script. If it were to be ad lib, I would probably be all right, but, if we had to read from a script, I was trapped. Somehow I had managed either to get out of any oral reading that the group had worked on that summer, or, as I had with the newspaper assignment, I had found a way to defuse the exercise. As a result, none of my cohorts knew that this was one of the areas, such as making introductions and talking on the telephone, where I could not maintain my show window fluency, my "only-a-mild-stutterer" disguise. I learned we were to read from a script and that I was to be on the program.

On the morning of the broadcast I knew what was going to happen. As I was eating breakfast, my stomach felt the way it had back in Miss Fielding's public speaking classes. During the program I had much more difficulty than anyone else in the group. I couldn't substitute words because each of us was holding an identical copy of the script. I went into all kinds of blocks and I was deeply embarrassed. I had asked a friend of mine to listen to the broadcast and count my blocks. In a hundred words I blocked fourteen times, often heavily. Joseph Sheehan was surprised. Later I heard he said about that day: "And there we had Fred Murray who was pretty fluent all summer, and then he went to pieces on the stutterers' broadcast."

I was low for the next day or so after that experience, but my embarrassed feelings didn't last. I was about to leave Iowa City, and on the whole I had had a wonderful experience there. Being part of that healthy, positive program had buoyed up my spirits, with a resulting improvement in my everyday speech, and I was feasting on that fluency. How ironic it was that this fluency, which I had gained in a program based on the acceptance of one's stuttering, encouraged my hopes for stutter-free speech!

Even after hearing it stated repeatedly all summer, I was only faintly able to appreciate the sense behind the Iowa philosophy. Marvelous as that program was, in eight short weeks nothing could have reversed my intense desire to conceal my stuttering. Almost everybody I had known and everything that had happened to me had told me that my handicap was something to be ashamed of. Such deeply emotional attitudes are not easily dislodged.

15

Introductions

By this time it was apparent to me that in spite of Dr. Johnson's discouraging words about a stutterer's chances in the field of speech pathology, many, possibly most, of the outstanding authorities on the subject of stuttering were stutterers themselves. Each of the major figures I had met—Mrs. Gifford and the Drs. Johnson, Sheehan, and Van Riper had suffered from the handicap, and, of the experts whose work I knew about from my reading and from the talk of speech clinicians, only Drs. Bryngelson and Travis were not stutterers.

It is obvious that a person's preoccupation with his own difficulty usually leads to his knowing a great deal about it. Once a degree of specialized knowledge on a subject has been accumulated, the possibility of sharing that knowledge arises naturally, along with the practical possibility of making a career in an area where he has active interest as well as a head start in information.

Another obvious reason for stutterers' making a specialty of stuttering is that the handicap tends to make a person retiring, and stutterers usually feel more comfortable in speech clinics than in the outside world. In one of the ASHA "Recovered" Stutterers' Panels, one participant said that was true in his case. He stayed in the world of a speech pathology student until he had a Ph.D., and then, he said, his stuttering suddenly became much more severe when he was about to go out into the world of normal speakers.

Dr. Sheehan has said that one stutterer can help another in ways that no normal-speaking therapist can. So it seems reasonable that there are advantages when the therapist is also a stutterer. There is often a special authority accorded within clinics to therapists or pathologists who have had personal experience with speech disability.

However, the reason that interests me the most as to why a stutterer becomes a speech pathologist is that he is trying to help himself in a mysterious predicament. When Dr. Van Riper was an adolescent, living in the upper peninsula of Michigan, he stood in front of a favorite birch tree on his family's land and made a pledge to that tree that someday he was going to find the answer to the problem of stuttering. He says he has to admit to that tree that so far he has failed. As I have written in Chapter 2, we still have only a few tentative answers to stuttering's origin, development, and "cure," and a stutterer who has the kind of curious mind that enjoys working on unsolved questions will have extra motivation to try to solve questions about stuttering.

Dr. Charles Bluemel, the famous speech authority and psychiatrist to whom I referred to in Chapter 1, told about becoming disgusted after going to what he called "quack" stuttering schools and not finding relief. About 1914 he went to the University of Colorado and read every book he could find in English, French, or German that dealt with speech disorders. He found information that seemed to him so dim and so hazy that he decided if he wanted to get better he would have to strike out for himself. I think this feeling has prompted many stutterers to enter the field.

■ ─── ■

I went back to Stanford in the fall of 1947 for my final semester. I finished my studies for a Bachelor of Arts degree in December, and then went into the Palo Alto hospital for the removal of a pilonidal cyst at the base of my spine. As a result of the spinal anesthetic and the general upheaval in my nervous system that having an operation creates, I had some difficulty talking while I was in the hospital, but the setback was a brief one, and I was soon able to speak as well as I had when I entered the hospital.

In March I went down to Los Angeles to look into the possibility of taking a Masters in Speech Pathology at the University of Southern California. I liked what I found there and made arrangements to begin work in the coming summer session.

As I was riding back on the train, I looked ahead in the car and saw a familiar-looking hat on the head of a woman who was sitting several rows ahead of me. That hat could only belong to Mabel Farrington Gifford. All of Mrs. Gifford's clothes were lovely. I think she must have had them made to order. In her studio she always wore chiffons and silks in light, relaxing shades of purple and blue. And her hats were fabulous. I always think of them as "My Fair Lady" hats, covered with bird feathers or flowers or fruit. This one had cherries and grapes surrounded by many leaves.

I got up and walked down the car, and, sure enough, it was Mrs. Gifford. She asked me to sit down beside her, and we chatted for more than an hour as the train sped toward San Francisco. I remember that my speech was good during our conversation. I don't remember blocking at all.

My father was going to meet me at the station with the car, and I thought how nice it would be if we could give Mrs. Gifford a ride up to her studio. But then I realized that this would mean I would have to introduce my father to Mrs. Gifford, and I couldn't face that. I was just too scared. So Mrs. Gifford rode the bus home.

That is a good example of my continuing avoidance behavior at the time. It is also a good example of a stutterer's fear of introductions. Most stutterers feel this. I would have had anxiety about introducing anybody on that train to my father, especially with a whole hour of anticipation to live through before we would meet him. But I suffered extreme anguish in introducing people I thought of as VIP's, and Mrs. Gifford was definitely an important person in my life. My having had therapy from her probably intensified the anxiety many times over what it would have been with an ordinary friend. I would have felt guilty and ashamed to have an obvious failure in front of her, and because the stakes were so high, the probability of my stuttering was practically one hundred percent.

Stutterers often get into trouble when they have a long time to worry about introductions they know are inescapably scheduled for the future. Paradoxically, stutterers also have trouble when the need to introduce two people comes unexpectedly, and in a flash of panic the stutterer's speech mechanism goes rigid. Dr. Van Riper has written that on such occasions the heartbeat has been known to reach 120 beats a minute within a matter of seconds. Behind both situations is the same pressure, the need to say certain words at a certain time, with no possibility of substitution. The words are, obviously, names, and the time problem exists because of social sensitivity. If I hesitate before saying a person's name, he may think I don't remember who he is or that he is worth remembering, and, if I hesitate before giving him my name, he may think I don't want to know him.

Introduction difficulty has never completely disappeared for me, although it is much easier now. Now I know how to direct my mechanism to prevent or modify such blocks. I have to get my thoughts organized. I have to wait a moment until I can think of the first person's name and hear it in my mind; then I have to think of and mentally hear the second name. It requires a search which I believe is longer than the search of a normal speaker who tends to get stuck on names, because I still have an emotional reaction that automatically inhibits my thought processes. I can't prevent the reaction, but I have learned how to surmount it. When I have both names clearly in my mind, I start in and deliberately speak the introduction. I can do it, but only after careful planning. I very seldom can leave it to chance.

When I know about an introduction ahead of time and have the names straight in my head, I can help myself further by focusing on keeping my speech muscles relaxed, so that if I do stutter it will be light, fluent stuttering.

A stutterer may try to work within the handicap, using his intelligence and imagination to ease situations that are unusually hard to get through; nevertheless, he will regularly come up against trials that seem inevitable. In 1971, long after my train ride with Mrs. Gifford, I arranged to have a number of important people in the speech field visit the University of New Hampshire. I had just built a house on the Oyster River in Durham, and the combination of guests and the new house prompted me to give a party. Because my guests were coming to speak at the university, I automatically added the names of the university president and his wife to my invitation list, never dreaming that they would accept. But lo and behold, they did. I began to think, "Oh, dear, here come the introductions!"

We know that severe stuttering blocks are often precipitated by a number of factors combining at a moment when speech is necessary. It is as though several forces are all coming together at one time in a funnel. Well, here in my funnel I could see combining the usual strain of introductions, plus the extra strain of introducing authorities whom I admired, plus all the social and domestic responsibilities involved in being a host, *plus* a housewarming!

I am often edgy when a party I am giving is about to begin, not just about the introductions, but also because I hate the early moments when the first guests come. They stand around, talking about the weather, and there's a terrible feeling of things not yet under way.

On the night of this party, six guests were standing in the living room when I looked out the window and saw the president and his wife coming up the walk. I thought, "Oh boy, now I've had it. I have to think of the names of all those people in there, and I'll have to introduce them, and I never can do it." I felt myself getting very flustered and tense, but I went to the door, opened it, and managed to smile and say "Hello."

From where they were standing, the president and his wife could look down the hall and see some of the guests sipping punch and talking, but, because I could feel my mouth tensing, I did not direct them toward the living room. Instead, I opened a door that connects the front hall with the back rooms of the house. Fighting to catch my breath and to get my speech mechanism ready to utter the necessary sounds, I took them through my bedroom, the bathroom, the guestroom, the laundry, and finally out into the kitchen. I must say they were marvelous. They showed no surprise at my leading them on this unusual tour, but made appreciative murmurs about this being handy and that being handsome, until at last I had exhausted all possible detours and the door from the kitchen to the living room was before us.

I pushed it open and we went through. The guests had stopped talking and were all standing facing the kitchen door. They must have been wondering what on earth I was doing and whether I had lost my mind.

I could not imagine myself getting through this thing smoothly, but I led the president and his wife up to the nearest woman. The sooner the ordeal started, the sooner it would be over. As I opened my mouth, the guest started to transfer her punch cup from the right to the left hand. In doing so she jerked a bit, out of nervousness, I suppose, and a fountain of dark purple wine punch went up into the air and down onto my new beige wall-to-wall wool carpeting.

It was the biggest "blockbuster" I have ever had. I didn't have to introduce anybody: They all met on their hands and knees, dabbing away at the stain with paper napkins while I ran back into the kitchen for cleaning fluid. The woman who had spilled the punch was nearly in tears. As I tried to still her apologies, I wished I could have told her what she had just done for me and given her a grateful hug. By the time the spot was gone, the ice was broken, and the party was underway.

16

USC

In June I went down to the University of Southern California (USC) to begin working on my master's degree in the field of Speech Correction, as it was then called, with an emphasis on audiometry, the testing of hearing. I may have been too stubborn to follow Dr. Wendell Johnson's advice entirely, but I had been impressed with the earnest way in which he tried to warn me about my prospects in the speech field, and I thought it prudent to begin in an area where I would not have to depend heavily on my speech.

One of my courses was called "The Psychology of Speech." It was taught by the head of the USC speech program, Dr. Lee Edward Travis. I already knew of the impressive work that Dr. Travis had done on cerebral dominance at The University of Iowa. I had read his 1931 book, *Speech Pathology*, a text that reflects, to this day, the brilliance of this scholarly man. In California, however, he was concentrating on something new. Every day I went to class to hear dynamic lectures in which he strongly urged deep psychotherapy as the best way out for the adult stutterer. He said that to treat only the symptoms of stuttering was equivalent to throwing a person with a fever into an ice box and saying "Cool off!"

Often Dr. Travis would spend several lectures on one remarkable case, describing the patient's free associations and the gradual improving of his speech during psychotherapy of the Freudian kind. Whereas, at the start of the therapy, the patient's stuttering had been full of contortions, after a year of sessions in which he lay on a couch and free-associated, saying everything that came into his mind, his stuttering became loose, without tension. Later, the free associations began to change, releasing more deeply repressed feelings, and the patient began to have periods as long as two weeks in which he stuttered very little. By the 285th hour, what happened to the stuttering? Bang!—Dr. Travis would hit one fist into his other hand—the stuttering seemed to go out the window! I sat there, thrilled, listening to this. Dr. Travis's dogmatic manner and his sharp lecture methods were very convincing. Almost everyone in the USC program at that time, including the doctoral candidates who were working under him, shared his enthusiasm.

Ever since my departure from USC in the early 1950's, I have kept in touch with Dr. Travis. I have come to appreciate, even more, the contributions this valued friend has made to the field. It is pleasing to me to note that, while he may continue to be supportive of psychotherapy as a present-day treatment for adult stutterers, he vigorously continues to reaffirm his theory of half a century ago that stuttering has an organic basis. I strongly agree with this concept.

■ ———————————————————————————————— ■

I was delighted when, at the beginning of the session, I heard that Dr. Wendell Johnson was bringing his family out to USC for the summer. He was going to teach a course in speech pathology at the university, and also do some speaking at other schools in the area. Although I was delighted for my own sake, I was somewhat concerned for Dr. Johnson, because I knew that he was not a supporter of analysis-oriented treatment for stuttering.

As it turned out, his beliefs were frequently challenged by USC people. His having to be in a somewhat defensive role probably explained the increased disfluency I noted in his speech during the summer session.

Apart from Dr. Johnson's theoretical disagreements with the USC staff, the Johnsons and I had a lot of fun during their time in California. Once, with other friends, we took a picnic lunch up to the top of Mt. Wilson. From the back seat of the car, I heard Dr. Johnson say he was going to take his family to San Francisco, so I said, "Wouldn't you like to stay at our house?"

He said, "Yes, we'd love to! I think we could do it!" and they did. They stayed three days. My parents enjoyed meeting them, and I took them sightseeing—over the Golden Gate Bridge, out to see the redwoods. We had a wonderful time.

■ ———————————————————————————————— ■

One Friday afternoon at USC, a speech pathologist gave a lecture on stuttering in Hancock Auditorium. There were four hundred people in the audience. The specialist, a woman, was the only speaker. She said at the outset that she used to stutter badly, and that if she should start to stutter during this lecture the audience should not be disturbed. She would simply handle it as best she could. But then she went through the speech easily, with only a few minor hesitations.

On the following Friday evening she was moderator for a forum at

UCLA, on the other side of the city. There she had to introduce a number of important people in the speech correction field, including Dr. Travis.

Again, there were about four hundred people in the audience. The pathologist came forward and said, "Good evening." She managed to say that all right, but then she just had a horrendous time. The words simply would not come out, and she chose to avoid going ahead until she felt she could release them. She stood there, whirling her hand about as though she were playing with a bunch of keys, trying to help herself time the moment when a word would come.

When a stutterer finds himself in a bad situation, it is only natural for him to resort to techniques that have helped him move forward in the past. In this instance, the speaker may have been using a timing movement similar to the arm swings that were taught in stuttering schools during the 1920's. At that time it was believed that such movements would help students with their speech rhythms.

At any rate, there she was, making her hand movements up on the stage, trying to hold back until the words would come. It made for a terribly slow, laborious beginning. She finally did get warmed up, but I was bewildered by the difference between her speech that night and the fluent way she had spoken in Hancock only one week before.

I think I understand most of it now. The difference reflected a difference in her role in the two situations, and a difference in the situations' communication pressure for her. At USC, she was the featured speaker. She had complete leeway about what she wanted to do, what she wanted to say, and when she would say it.

At UCLA she faced the psychological pressure that every stutterer feels when he is forced to appear with normal speakers. And I suppose there was extra pressure resulting from the fame of the panel members.

But I am sure that the chief reason for her difficulty on the second Friday was that at UCLA she was not in control. She was in a position where she had to say precise things at precise times, with those words to a great extent determined by the other people there. Immediately after one speaker finished, she was obliged to get up, thank him, and begin to introduce the next speaker by saying his name and something about him. It may seem paradoxical, but those time and content requirements actually made the UCLA chairman role a much more demanding one for her than the USC task of holding the interest of four hundred people for more than an hour, and doing it all alone.

Those two performances have always seemed to me to demonstrate most clearly the momentary effect of role and communication pressure upon a stutterer's speech.

In the fall of 1948 I took a course called "Introduction to Speech Correction" that Conrad Wedberg was teaching at USC. He had marvelous speech in those lectures—I believe he didn't stutter once all semester. In class he said repeatedly that he thought a stutterer could not hope for improvement until he had come to terms with his own feelings. Like Mrs. Gifford, Mr. Wedberg felt that it was necessary for an adult stutterer to think back to rediscover and release his early conflicts and repressed emotions. In the process, Mr. Wedberg said, his stuttering personality would be transformed into a nonstuttering one. Mr. Wedberg was not against psychoanalysis as a help in accomplishing this task.

In speaking about his own improvement, he often said, "I stuttered because I felt the way I felt." I agree about the close relationship between a stutterer's state of mind and the state of his speech. However, I think a theory that calls for the control of one's speech through control of emotions is vulnerable because emotions are often terribly hard to control. Along with self-understanding and good mental hygiene, I believe that a stutterer needs mechanical aids such as the prolongation to arm himself for the times when pressure appears.

When Mr. Wedberg talked about those pressured times when emotions get out of hand, he said that there was nothing to do but to wait until the turbulent feelings subsided of their own accord. He thought this process could not be hurried; however I have found that a fast walk or a swim—some kind of strenuous exercise—will frequently help to release my own thoughts from a preoccupation that has started up a panic.

■ ———————————————————————————————— ■

I was glad I had decided to go down to USC. I was studying material that interested me, and my grades were the best they had ever been. My Iowa experience had given me more confidence, along with greater knowledge in the field of speech correction.

A bonus for me in my USC situation was the nearby presence of an aunt, who lived with her husband in San Marino. Her husband was the headmaster of a Pasadena school. The three of us had many pleasant evenings together while I was at USC. I went out for a visit with them nearly every week. Later, in 1953, when I went down to say goodbye to them before leaving for my army tour in Japan, it turned out to be one of the few occasions in my life when something besides stuttering prevented my being able to speak.

■ ———————————————————————————————— ■

In addition to my academic work, I joined several extracurricular groups at USC. One of these comes to my mind whenever I am asked if a listener should provide the word that a stutterer is obviously struggling to say.

The activity was a series of dancing lessons, which turned out to be taught by a stutterer. He used to arrange the eight of us in pairs in a line at one end of his studio, put a record on the phonograph, and then demonstrate a new step. The record was often a song called "Rain," ". . . pitter patter on the pane," it continued, and we would all go together toward the far wall, practicing what he had showed us.

When we reached the wall, we would mark time, one foot up and one foot down, waiting for his signal to reverse and start back again. Occasionally he could pop it out fairly fast, but most of the time it would be thirty seconds before he could say, "Turn around." Every time I hear that song I have an immediate flashback image of our teacher severely blocking, his lips pursed, his head thrown back in contortions, and our feet going up and down to the melody of "Rain."

Well, what should we have done? I suppose we could have turned on our own when we got to the wall, but we weren't sure what the next instructions would be. Sometimes he would give us a new step at that point, and it seemed best just to stand there and mark the time.

Most stutterers do resent having words said for them, and usually they should not be helped. The best course for the listener to take is to show by courteous attention that he understands the stutterer is in trouble, that the stuttering is not interfering with their relationship, and that he, the listener, is willing to wait patiently until the stutterer is able to speak for himself. Stutterers feel defeated when their listeners talk for them. While, in general, it is better to let the stutterer keep the communication responsibility, if the communication is very urgent, the listener may, of course, have to provide the word.

■ ───────────────────────────────────── ■

In the spring of 1949 I signed up for "Clinical Methods," a required course in which the students worked with youngsters who had speech problems. Since the administrators of the USC program at that time were convinced that stuttering was a symptom of emotional repression, they gave me, a stutterer who had not had psychotherapy, the two cases with the fewest emotional complications. One was a boy of twelve who was hard of hearing, and the other was a boy of five who had a cleft palate.

As part of standard therapist training, we had to telephone the parents of our cases, to make appointments and to talk about the children's progress. My first call was to the mother of Tommy, the five year old. I postponed making that call for two days, thinking about it almost continually. When I finally picked up the phone, I was in a state of extreme physical and mental tension, and, when Tommy's mother answered, I blocked very badly. I did get my message out, but I did it with enormous difficulty, and the poor woman must have had an anxiety attack of her own. I later discovered that she called the clinic director and asked who this man could be who had phoned her, who couldn't talk at all himself. She said she didn't want me working with her boy.

The director replied that, although I was a stutterer, I didn't stutter when I was with small children, and I wouldn't contaminate her son. Somehow he convinced her. I went on working with Tommy, in the process doing things such as taking him out and playing with him in the sandbox, and I had no difficulty speaking to him at all.

My supervisor volunteered to call the parents of my other case for me, and, at the end of the semester, the administrators arranged to have a senior therapist present at my meetings with the children's parents. She did most of the talking. My friends at USC were good to me in these situations, but the message I was getting was plain. My stuttering was, at times, still so bad that unless I could find a way to improve further it was going to jeopardize my chances in my chosen field. My instructors urged me to try an analytic type of therapy.

At this time the USC doctoral candidates were using analytic-type therapy with stutterers who had come to the USC clinic for help. The speech pathology department was in an army barracks that was left over from the war. On the second floor of this building was a small room containing a cot, a table, and a lamp, and it was there that the therapists would sit to hear the free associations of their cases.

The overwhelming curiosity and enthusiasm at USC about this treatment was infectious. We used to stand around in the clinic and say things such as "Let's see. That man's had about forty hours and he's still stuttering some. Now that woman coming down the stairs has had about ninety hours. Have you heard her stutter lately?"

One of the doctoral students who was about to begin private practice tried to persuade me to become his patient, saying, "Fred, if you know anybody who wants to get better, who really wants to get better, to lick his stuttering, let me know." He put so much pressure on me he made me angry.

I thought, "Oh no, buddy, you're not going to get me on your couch!"

But I had begun to think that analysis might work its wonders for me. In early September of 1949 I went at 9:30 A.M. to the office of a highly recommended, established psychologist to discuss his taking me on for treatment. I sat there and waited until almost noon. I guess he was testing me to see if I could wait, to see how seriously I wanted treatment.

Whatever his reason, I stuck it out and he said he thought he could find some hours for me. He was very frank. He said this wouldn't be like an operation in which if the knife slips the patient might die. But, he said, we were going to go into some pretty deep areas, since stuttering itself was a very deep disorder. There was no guarantee of a cure, but he said he had found analysis of the Freudian type, using free association, to be the best possible therapy for the adult stutterer.

I left his office bursting with expectation. Something new was about to be done. I was in the hands of an expert. My cure was going to be complete.

17

Analysis

Over the next thirty-two months my analyst and I met three times a week during the school year. When we stopped we had spent 250 hours together. I lay on a couch in a small room which was wallpapered with a pattern of yellow roses, and he sat on a chair behind and to the right of my head. He told me to close my eyes and imagine that I was looking at a blank movie screen. I was to report everything that I saw or felt.

Most people know how free association works. The first thoughts a person has are of apparently irrelevant things, and then patterns begin to emerge that have significance for him. Members of his family and close friends appear frequently. Emotions such as hostility and desire are expressed.

The only consciously structured image I ever reported in my analysis was the first one. Because I felt so optimistic about the outcome of this treatment, I wanted to start it off with a little ceremony. I said, "The very first thing I want to see is the Hyde Street Ferry Pier in San Francisco. There is a ferryboat at that pier. I'm coming down Hyde Street hill. I'm going aboard. This boat is sailing, and it represents the start of the analysis." I even said something like "Here's a bottle of champagne to send it off."

The image of a ferryboat is one that appeared repeatedly in my later free associations, originating in real life with the boats I watched as a child in San Francisco Bay. Boats are commonly associated with freedom, with getting away from one's normally confining life. My stuttering often confined me to silence when I wanted to speak, and when I was younger it kept me from trying many things that I wanted to do, so I suppose it was not surprising that boats and voyage images were active in my subconscious mind.

In a later association, the ferryboat pier seemed to be the mouthpiece of a telephone. There was a tube running for three or four miles just under the surface of the water from this mouthpiece to another pier on the opposite shore. The tube was clogged with sewage. Standing at the mouthpiece, I became angry at the tube's plugged condition. I seemed to have enormous power. I blew with all my strength through that line until it was completely clear.

In accordance with the Freudian tradition, my analyst did not give me specific interpretations of any of my associations. He did tell me that I was one of the most prolific free associators that he had ever encountered. I flowed so fast that he could not keep written notes on everything I said. I felt no inhibition or fear, even though I was often talking about people or situations that in the real world frightened me. In that situation I could even imagine using the telephone without feeling afraid.

Although I know that during analysis other stutterers have experienced terrible blocking when they reached matters about which they were emotional, my speech throughout these sessions was the most fluent it had ever been. I can recall only one time that I actually blocked significantly. I was in a frame of mind where I just didn't want to talk. Perhaps I was resisting something I didn't want to recognize. I stuttered then, but in a loose way without any tension. My fluency came, I believe, from my faith in the doctor, and from the nonjudgmental nature of the situation I was in. Within that room I felt no threats. I was really alone with myself.

Just as the analyst rarely commented on or asked questions about any of my associations, he almost never had anything to say about my dreams, which he asked me to write down. I kept paper, a pen, and a flashlight by my bed, and, whenever I would wake from a dream, I would write it down. At the start of our next session, I would hand the pages over to the doctor. He'd read them, and then he'd say something like "Uh! Let's start today free associating from the point in the dream where you see yourself inside the nasturtium blossom." And off I'd go.

He told me that he thought I was not a severe stutterer so far as the overt symptoms were concerned, but that my emotional problems which resulted from stuttering were severe. I think he was right. All the avoiding, suppressing patterns I had been following were really repressive, burying much of the violence of my feelings about my stuttering as I hid the symptoms. On the pressured occasions when my stuttering did erupt, it was unusually severe because my violent feelings surfaced with it. A large part of my later improvement came when my anger about being a stutterer began to diminish.

After hearing at USC Dr. Travis's examples of stuttering improvement during analysis, I expected that after nine months of treatment, when we stopped for the summer vacation of 1950, my stuttering would be dramatically improved. When summer came, however, I could not see that my speech was any better in the cue situations where I always met trouble. If anything, my stuttering under those circumstances was worse. I was still so impressed by the enthusiasm in the USC clinic for analysis, and I still had so much faith in my analyst, that my lack of improvement did not bother me very much. I told myself that I had to be patient, that progress with this treatment was apparently not continuous. Perhaps it was more like a series of plateaus that were interrupted by regressions.

I had received my master's degree in January, 1950, and then I stayed on in Los Angeles, working at a hearing center there and continuing the therapy. I went home for the summer of 1950. I had learned that my mother had a serious, progressive illness. Her death did not occur until the summer of 1952, and, before it came, she went through many critical periods in which her illness caused much discomfort. Whenever we could, my father, my brother, and I tried to be with her.

Once during those last years she said to me, "Well, you've got so much better that even if you don't make any further headway, I know I don't have to worry about you anymore. You are fluent enough." She was talking about the casual speech she heard from me every day, and while I knew that I still had a long way to go before I could be satisfied, I was deeply happy to hear her say those words.

■ ——————————————————————————————————— ■

I went back to Los Angeles in the fall of 1950 to work at the hearing center and to continue the analysis. In the summer of 1951 I was offered a job working in the summer rehabilitation therapy program at the College of the Pacific in Stockton, some eighty miles east of San Francisco. There were to be six groups of handicapped youngsters in the program, some hard of hearing, some with cerebral palsy, some slow learners, and so on, and I was to be in charge of the seven stutterers, whose ages ranged from ten to sixteen. The program was to last five weeks. I was to teach five days a week, Monday through Friday, and the pay would be $350. The offer suited me particularly well because I needed to be near home. So I took the job, went down to Stockton, and found a room in a house there. All summer long, whenever I heard the phone ring in that house, I feared it was bad news for me about my mother. But she held on, and the call never came.

By 1951, with the help of the prolongation and my other mechanical skills, most of the time I appeared to be fluent. In talking to my group of young, mostly severe, stutterers I did not stutter. And I did everything I could to keep things that way. Whenever an activity came up in which I feared I might stutter, I managed to avoid it. Once, when we were reading a story, the youngsters said, "Come on, Mr. Murray, read some of this to us." I refused. I knew I would stutter, and I was ashamed to have my charges, whom I was supposed to be helping, hear me do it.

I was elated one day when the head of the program said to me, "You know, Murray, you've been here three weeks and I haven't heard you stutter once!" That set me up for hours. I foolishly thought I had achieved a triumph. Actually, in my compulsion to make everyone at Stockton that summer think of me as a non-stutterer, I was inflicting an increasing strain on myself that could only end with defeat. Full of pride, I was putting all my money on a horse called fluency. If he won, I won, but it had to be a short-lived triumph because in other races he was bound to lose.

Fluency didn't win, but maybe he placed or showed in the middle of the fourth week, when I had to make a short report on my group's progress to the other therapists at an evening meeting. That night I had dinner at the home of a friend in Stockton. I remember the sick apprehension which stayed with me during the meal, fear that I was going to stutter. I went to the meeting, very tight in my stomach. When my turn to speak came, I managed to get out my few words without actually blocking, but I did falter a little, and afterward the director stopped me at the door, slapped me on the back, and said loudly, "Well, I caught you tonight! First time I heard you fluff!" Of course, my face went scarlet, and my pride went down to sell for about five cents a share.

If I thought that little meeting was a problem, I should have known what was coming next. The following day the director called us all together and said, "Now at the end of the summer session we're going to have a finale. There's going to be a get-together with the parents and the administration at one of the fraternity houses, and I want each of your groups to be there." We were all going to perform. Each of the group heads was to make a speech. All the bells of warning began to ring inside my head.

In a situation like that one, when a stutterer knows that on a certain day in the future he is going to have to speak under pressure, there is a feeling similar to one we all have experienced when the first clouds of a bad thunderstorm appear on the horizon. The first anxiousness, when the scene is still calm, is mild but unmistakable. There is something ahead that is negative. As the clouds grow larger and darker, the anxiety increases, and, as the moment of the first huge boom and lightning flash comes near, there is a strong, panicky surge of claustrophobia, the inevitability of a crisis, the impossibility of escape.

And so, all week long I thought about trying to live up to the role of the teacher, the expert who knows how to help stutterers be fluent. I thought of myself as a teacher standing before the parents who had paid for his services and who would therefore be especially critical of the way he could speak. I thought of the college administration people who would be there, making judgments, and I thought of my fellow therapists listening, and then I thought of the director who would be in a somewhat defensive position since he had hired me for the job. I couldn't eat.

I barely slept. And, my terror grew. I couldn't see how I could keep my show window speech going through the strain of that finale.

Well, of course, the night came. The anxiety was overwhelming. We went to the fraternity house, which had two large downstairs rooms connected by a wide hall. The audience, about seventy people, were gathered in the living room, and we, the performers, were assembled in the dining room waiting to be called in. I remember hearing the director of our program making his welcoming speech. Waves of apprehension began passing over me, fear so violent I felt as though I were back in junior high school again, about to begin my disastrous 1940 assembly speech.

When the program director finished his greeting, he called in group number one. The leader of that group went out with his children into the living room to perform. My group was number three.

I had a friend among the therapists there whose name was Margaret. She was the therapist in charge of the hard of hearing. Margaret was a Christian Scientist, and, during our conversations that summer she had repeatedly said to me, "Fred, you've got to realize the importance of the Truth. If you can see the Truth, you'll be free."

Standing there, knowing I was going to be called on next, I suddenly saw Margaret waiting with her group on the other side of the dining room. I was desperate, and I called to her as loudly as I dared, over the heads of the others, "Margaret! Margaret!"

She looked over at me and then asked, "What?"

"Margaret!" I said, "The Truth! The Truth!" I wanted her to throw me the Truth, which would, like a life preserver, rescue me from a sea in which I was drowning.

I don't think Margaret ever understood what it was I wanted. She smiled at me as though I were making a joke. I heard the director saying, "And now we're going to hear from Mr. Frederick Murray. Mr. Murray holds an M.A. in Speech Correction from the University of Southern California. He's an expert on stuttering, and we are fortunate to have him on our staff."

I walked into that room like a condemned man walking his last thirteen steps. My blue shirt was dark with sweat. I could not seem to get the speech mechanism going. In this state, using either the prolongation or the bounce was impossible. My cheeks puffed out, my lips and tongue protruded, my head jerked with the effort as, finally, one word bursting out after another, I slowly exploded my way through the first words. Blocking continually, the veins standing out on my forehead, I managed to call my first little boy forward, and then, somehow, the others after him. They all spoke far better than I did. I could not bring myself to look at any of their faces.

Finally, the evening was over. The director was at the door, handing out paychecks. I just pushed past him, taking my check out of his hand, hardly saying thank you. I ran out to my car, turned the key forcefully, and pumped the accelerator so hard that the gears shrieked. When I got the car going, I cranked the steering wheel as far around as it would go, tore out of the parking lot, got the car up to full speed, and escaped from that town. I never have gone back.

■ ———————————————————————————————————— ■

If I could speak to that twenty-five-year-old Fred Murray today, I would try to convince him not to set such devastating requirements for himself. In earthquake-prone cities, because of the earth's periodic shaking, buildings can only be built so high. In stuttering therapy, we learn to hold down our expectations for our speech behavior, not to build a tower of pride so high that it will be especially vulnerable to the shakings that are inevitable in every stutterer's experience.

Before Fred Murray went to Stockton, I would have said to him: "Okay, you're going to have this job for five weeks. Somehow, early, you're going to have to make sure that those around you hear you stutter, even if you have to fake a little. Establish yourself as a good therapist for stutterers, who sometimes stutters himself. See how your occasional stuttering might make your students feel closer to you (rather than making them think less of you), and how your usual fluency with them would encourage their hopes for themselves all the more."

When he first heard about the finale, I wish I could have said to him: "Recognize ahead of time how full of difficult elements for you that night will be. The entire summer has been a tense one because of your mother's illness. At the finale, even though you have been relieved of the need to speak perfectly, there will still be unusual strains, including the old problem of introducing your students, of having to say specific words at a specific time. Adult audiences are especially hard to speak to, particularly ones that include people in authority. Remember, in the well-known *Book of Lists*, which gives the highest to lowest, largest to smallest, etc., lists of significant items—the fear of speaking to an audience is listed as the greatest fear possessed by an average person!

"See if you can arrange your introduction to make room for your possible stuttering. At the start of your speech you might refer to your having been a severe stutterer. Or, you might make a joke about it, to ease tension on that subject both for yourself and for your listeners. The parents will know you are a stutterer because their children will have told them. You might even speak briefly but directly to the parents about the relationship between tension and stuttering. In every way you can, try to reduce the pressure on yourself to the point where you can be free enough to think about what you want to say, rather than the way in which you are going to be able to say it.

"And then decide ahead of time that, even if you stutter all the way through your speech, you are not going to let it be a total loss for yourself, but that you will do your best to maintain an experimental attitude toward your performance, a kind of curious objectivity, in which you watch yourself and see what you can learn from the experience. This attitude will help to lessen your feeling of being a victim.

"When you're scared and you fail, the experience is seen only as a blur: You just feel you're hurtling through it. But, with this preset attitude of inquiry, it is possible to look at what is happening almost as though you are slowing down a movie, studying what is happening, trying to see where your major obstacles are, so that another time you can find a way to handle them.

"Finally, as W. S. Merwin says in his poem 'Teachers,' 'Remember your unimportance,' and do not exaggerate the importance of this evening. No one's life depends on your stuttering or not stuttering there. No matter how the finale goes, the next day will come. In the meantime, apply an adhesive to the wound of your battered ego and return to your role as a participant in life's challenges."

■ ─── ■

Even though the Stockton debacle had made me wonder what all those expensive hours of free association were doing for my speech, I returned to Los Angeles, resumed psychotherapy in September, and continued with it until its conclusion in May of 1952. During that period I went to San Francisco often to see my mother, and, after May, I returned there to live at home for the last twelve weeks of my mother's life.

Someone once said that trying to define and to assess the results of psychoanalysis is like trying to nail a custard pie to the wall; but one positive result of my therapy of which I am sure is that it prepared me for those last weeks of my mother's life. My speech held together that summer, and I was able to be a support to both parents, helping my father take care of necessary household matters at that difficult time. In *The Treatment of Stuttering*, Dr. Van Riper has written that one of the three aims of psychotherapy is "to increase the person's ability to tolerate stress." I do believe that my analysis helped me in this respect.

Another improvement which I credit to the analysis was a marked drop in the attention I paid to social status. It was a relief to begin to let go of the assumptions about social superiority which I had been taught as a child and which were so important to my family. Since 1952, my tolerance for different kinds of behavior has grown, and I hope, and believe, I have become less judgmental in my thoughts as well as in my conversation.

Another of Dr. Van Riper's aims of psychotherapy is "to develop self-esteem and social adequacy," and in this respect, too, I think I profited from the analysis. Since no moral assessments were made of whatever murk I dredged up in those free associations, I stopped worrying about whether I were good or bad, normal or abnormal. All by itself, the sheer volume of hours and attention that I directed toward my own thoughts reinforced my sense of my own existence. The repetitive patterns that emerged from the associations were representations of my essential self. I liked many of them. Many of them reminded me of strong interests that I wanted to take up or continue to pursue. A positive spirit of self-acceptance grew steadily, and, as this happened, my defensive worries about what other people thought of me diminished. I felt substantial enough in my own being that I did not need the approval of society to make me feel all right about myself.

That does not mean I didn't care what anybody thought of me. I cared very much about the opinions of people whom I admired, people in my own field, and people whom I was trying to help. I cared what everybody at that Stockton finale thought of me, and that is probably why I had such a terrible time there.

Dr. Van Riper's third aim of psychotherapy is "to relieve distressing anxiety and its related symptoms." For my purposes, the word "symptom" here means stuttering. Probably many old sources of anxiety were weakened as their importance for me diminished in the process I have just described. But, unfortunately, the kind of analysis I received did nothing to help me diminish either my anxiety in many situations about which I felt real concern, or, more importantly, the irrational, extreme anxiety that overwhelmed me in response to cue situations such as the telephone, introductions, and specific speech.

In real life, stuttering usually occurs in response to real pressure and to the real cues about which the stutterer has developed neurotic fear. In analysis, references to these pressures and cues may not raise anxiety because the stutterer knows they are not real. On the couch he is totally safe. I could talk and talk about the telephone during analysis without feeling the slightest degree of fear. I could even pretend to speak on the phone. If I had had a toy telephone, I doubt that anything would have happened. Only if the analyst had brought a real telephone into the room and asked me to make an important phone call in front of him would I have had anxiety, and then it would have been real. But, then I would not have been having analytic therapy; I would have been undergoing a behaviorist form of treatment.

A large part of stuttering behavior occurs in response to a feeling that some harm is approaching the person. He feels threatened, and he feels on the defensive. The clinicians in Iowa talked about oversatisfying one's fear, which means doing something fearful because it induces stuttering, and doing it over and over until the experience begins to lose its power. Today we use the word "deconditioning" for the same process. It is extremely difficult in analysis to decondition a stutterer's fear response to his cues because he knows that the electrical switchboard he is talking about, playing with, and taking apart has been disconnected.

Then, stuttering is, in part, a deeply conditioned habit involving incorrect use of the physical speech mechanism. Today behavior modification therapies have little or nothing to do with emotions. At times speech is pre-planned. Facial muscles are voluntarily loosened. The stutterer learns new, relaxed ways to speak, with the hope that the new habits will become automatic. While these therapies can be faulted for leaving the emotions to adjust by themselves to the new physical state, they are having sufficiently impressive results to indicate that certain stutterers can benefit from at least some therapy of this kind. Analysis is not concerned with the physical speech mechanism.

Joseph Sheehan once told me that he thought the time and money that I put into analysis was wasted. He said I would have been better off if I had spent that period working actively on my speech instead of deliberately putting myself into a vacuum beyond the main line of the problem, lying down and talking about hypothetical things.

In many ways I agree with him. I am not anti-analysis. I support it for various problems, and I think it was somewhat strengthening for me. But, I do not support it as a therapy for stuttering, unless the person has such a disturbed personality that he needs to go through analysis to clear the way before speech therapy can take hold. Occasionally we see hysterical stuttering, stuttering which begins suddenly and has an emotional cause, and, of course, some kind of psychotherapy would be in order in this instance.

However, it probably would not be the Freudian type of therapy, in which the therapist does not respond verbally to his patient's imaginings, dreams, and ideas—even to his questions. This aspect of analysis was infuriating for me, as it has been for numerous others who have gone through it. It seems then to be a shocking waste of time and money. Many analysts, who formerly practiced Freudian analysis are now using much more of a reality-testing, face-to-face kind of therapy in which the analyst and his patient talk together most of the time about current difficulties. Penetrating the mists of the past is not as central to therapy as it used to be. How helpful it would have been if I had had a doctor talk to me the way I theoretically addressed the young Fred Murray who was about to leave for Stockton! My former analyst told me recently that he now uses this approach. I believe Dr. Travis now favors it, also.

How much did the analysis improve my speech? I can only say it was somewhat improved. One reason the improvement is hard to measure is that my ordinary speech was already good. The analysis did not change my disgust for my stuttering, or my dream of a complete cure. Those were two areas where I now know I badly needed help. But, worse, as I went off to the army in November of 1952, my drastic responses to cue situations were as strong as ever.

18

Army Life

One day in 1952 I was shocked to receive an order to report for an army physical. When I had registered for the draft back in 1943, I had been classified 4-F because of my stuttering. At the time of the Korean conflict it never occurred to me that I might be taken.

If someone had asked me if I wanted to be drafted, I would have said no. The prospect of fighting in Korea lacked the glamorous spirit of adventure and crusade that I had felt about World War II. Many of my classmates had not returned from that war, and some of the allies that they had fought for seemed to be our enemies in 1952. I had finished my master's degree, and I was enjoying my work at the Metropolitan Hearing Center in Los Angeles.

When I arrived at the induction center, a major with medical insignia on his lapel examined my folder.

"Murray, according to this, you are a stutterer. Is that right?"

"Yes."

"Excuse me, Murray. I couldn't hear you."

"Yes," I repeated.

"Yes what, Murray?"

"Yes, I . . ." (I expected to block on the usually troublesome "I," but it didn't happen.) "I occasionally stutter. Not nearly as badly as I used to, but I still stutter."

The major looked at me quizzically.

"I realize, sir, that that's a strange statement to make when I am speaking normally, but the fact is that once in a while I sound more like a badly tuned engine than a human being." (Where was my affliction now that I could use it? And why was I babbling on like this?)

"So you do stutter, is that it?"

"Yes, sir. I do stutter."

"Well, we'll be sure to give you a job where you won't have to talk very much." He stamped my folder and handed it back to me. The stamp read "1-A."

Six weeks later, when I received my orders to report for active duty, I cursed for five minutes with perfect fluency. I was assigned to basic training at San Luis Obispo, two hundred miles south of San Francisco.

My unit commander, a sergeant, processed his new recruits individually.

"Name?" he asked, when my turn came.

"Mu-Mu-Mu-Murray." I answered.

"Mu-Mu-Mu-Murray?" he asked.

"Ye-ye-ye-yes."

It became one of his routines. "Mu-Mu-Mu-Murray, would you mind picking up your ri-ri-ri-rifle and showing me how quickly you can break it do-do-do-down? Thank you, Mu-Mu-Mu-Murray."

This kind of good-natured ridicule didn't bother me very much. What I did mind were the occasions on which I stuttered in front of my peers, particularly when we were lined up for roll call at four in the morning. A sergeant would sound off with a last name, and that soldier was supposed to come up with his first name, middle initial, and serial number fast. The sergeant would shout "King!" and King would shoot back his own first name, middle initial, and serial number. "Murray!" There would be a long pause, gurglings, some snickering from the other men, and then finally my "F-F-F-F-F-Frederick P., U.S. f-f-five, six, two, zero, zero, e-e-e-e-eight, four, two."

So, there were some embarrassing times. But, for the most part, I adopted the philosophy that since the army had elected to take me, it had to take me, defects and all. Nothing is very serious in the army, at least for the enlisted man during basic training. I did my jobs, got my pay, and shot the breeze with the other men, using appropriately spaced expletives in the military fashion. I surrendered most of my initiative taking to Uncle Sam, knowing he would support me for two years and would give me three meals a day whether I stuttered or not.

On one occasion I had to stay behind and report to the inspecting officer when he came around in the morning that the barracks were ready for inspection. In this instance I didn't care whether or not I stuttered. When I did stutter and the officer looked at me strangely, it didn't seem important.

My unit left the port of San Francisco for Japan on the old troop ship *General Mitchell*. As I watched the skyline of the city fading away, I could see the outline of the house I had grown up in, which was then about to be sold. One day, I thought, I will look back fondly at my days in basic training. I had never before felt part of a large group for so sustained a time. I had enjoyed the relaxed humor in most of my exchanges with the other men. I suppose it reflected our general helplessness in determining our immediate fates, along with an unusually strong sense of the ephemeral nature of life. I think, too, that I had been trying to force an end to my stuttering, and it was a relief to have to relinquish most of that effort for a while. It was also a relief to be temporarily taken away from the speech world where my problem was always before me.

When we landed in Yokohama eleven days later, the troops filed smartly off the ship, with a nearly perfect ten feet between each man. Every man stopped at the end of the gangplank, shouted off his name and serial number, then marched on to take his place in a line that was forming farther down the dock. When my turn came, I blocked on my name. By the time I got it out, there was a gap of at least one hundred feet between me and the man ahead.

Our orders were given out. I was assigned to an army stockade in Nakano, a part of Tokyo. One of my jobs there was lecturing to groups of transient prisoners who were G.I.'s, explaining how they should fill out the forms that were required of every prisoner who was entering or leaving. I stuttered so badly giving those talks that some of the prisoners were irritated. Aware of it, I turned the task over to my assistant, an honor prisoner. At first I didn't mind sitting on the sidelines, but then I became disgusted with myself. With so much education and therapy behind me, why couldn't I handle this myself?

When the next group came in, I told the assistant I would give the lecture. He said, "But, you can't, Mr. Murray, you'll stutter." I said that I didn't care. Of course, I did stutter at first, but I kept working, and, after two weeks of determined effort, I got that speech so improved that practically none of the prisoners who came in subsequently knew I was a stutterer. I used some mechanical aids to help me, and I rearranged some of the words so that the speech would be easier; however, the most important factor in that improvement was the switch in my own attitude, from a defensive one to an aggressive one.

Conrad Wedberg has written that the voice of a stutterer says "I don't believe in myself." Earlier, when I gave my lecture over to my assistant, I wasn't believing in myself. Then, when I got mad at myself, I got organized, believing I could do it, and went right ahead and solved that problem.

From that time on, my speech in the service was generally good. There were a few unexpected relapses, though, and one of these occurred one night when I was left in charge of Cell Block One. The telephone rang just as the head sergeant came back into the room. I picked it up and tried to say "Block One, Private Murray speaking," but I blocked completely on the "One."

"Block wa-wa-wa-wa-wa . . ." I tried, going on for what seemed like minutes. The sergeant stood there with his fists on his hips, looking at me. Then, thoroughly annoyed, he picked up my logbook and slammed it down on the desk. The crash released my block. "One!" I said easily, and then I looked at the sergeant and thanked him. He grabbed the phone and glared at me in a way that left no doubt about my place in his military heart.

■ ———————————————————————————————————— ■

Many stutterers have found that some kind of physical jarring will successfully release a word on which they are blocking, as that book's slamming released my "One." In the BBC television series, "I, Claudius," viewers saw the Emperor Claudius break his stuttering blocks by slapping his own arm or his knee.

The trouble with distractions of this kind is that they lose their power. When I was studying at Harvard, I knew a stutterer who found he could break his blocks by stamping on the floor. It worked for a while, but then he found he had to stamp harder and longer to release a word. Finally, the whole house in which he lived seemed to shake from his pounding. The students who shared that house with him asked him either to stop speaking late at night and during study times or to find a quieter way of distracting himself out of a block.

In the 1968 ASHA "Recovered" Stutterers' Panel, one speaker said that to break his stuttering blocks he had tried foot patting, eye blinking, and arm waving, and that they had turned him into a foot-patting, eye-blinking, arm-waving stutterer, but a stutterer nevertheless. He said he had learned that all such crutches eventually will fail the stutterer, sometimes when they are being counted on the most. Stutterers will fare better if they ignore the temptations that those devices present and work at finding a way to deal with the stuttering behavior itself.

■ ———————————————————————————————————— ■

It was at the suggestion of Dr. Wendell Johnson that I made several trips to observe therapy that was being conducted in two private schools in Tokyo. One of these schools was run, in large part, by the late Sachiyuki Hamamoto, then in his twenties. I encouraged him to improve his English and then come to the United States to work for clinical certification by ASHA. After he had successfully accomplished this, he returned to Japan, where he spent the remainder of his years setting up clinics there and in Hong Kong.

Some months after visiting the schools, I became interested in finding out what luck Japanese doctors were having with a treatment in which stutterers were injected with the drug scopolamine. The drug made the stutterers so drowsy that its use seemed impractical to me. Nevertheless, I enjoyed talking to the clinicians and seeing what else was going on in the schools. Later, I wrote an article about these therapy schools and medical clinic visits for a 1958 issue of ASHA's *Journal of Speech and Hearing Disorders*.

Dr. Johnson also wrote to me about an Indian stutterer who had written to him from Calcutta. He asked me to visit that man for him, if I were going to visit India while I was in the Far East. I had already begun to think that I would like to remain in Japan for a time after I became a civilian, and then do some traveling on my way home. I wrote Dr. Johnson that I could see the Indian stutterer and made arrangements to end my tour of duty and to sail in November, 1954, from Yokohama on the German cargo-passenger liner *Schwabenstein*.

The author on the right with Lt. Frank Vondrasek and Pvt. Allen Redring at Camp San Luis Obispo, 1953.

19

Around the World

And so that November I embarked on a year-long trip in which my personal and professional interests were continually intertwined. As traveling has always been one of my favorite pastimes, on the European part of this trip I was able to combine pleasure and education, because almost everywhere I went I visited institutions that treated stutterers. I was looking for methods which, as a pathologist, I could someday use to help other stutterers; and, of course, I was still looking for my own magical cure. When I returned to California in October of 1955, I had been around the world. I had visited more than sixteen countries, and I had seen in use almost that many different therapy treatments for stuttering.

The *Schwabenstein*'s first stop was the Japanese city of Kobe where, to my surprise and pleasure, the ship was boarded briefly by my Japanese friend, Sachiyuki Hamamoto, who had come from Tokyo to say goodbye.

Then the ship went on to the Philippines, to Hong Kong, and to Singapore, where I left it to fly to Calcutta. Dr. Johnson's Indian correspondent had sounded desperate in his letter, but when I met the man in a Calcutta hotel, his stuttering did not strike me as severe. He did, however, suffer from great anxiety about it. In some ways my evaluation of his condition was like the one my analyst had, much earlier, made of me.

We talked about the shame that an Indian family feels when one of its members is a stutterer and about the special humiliation known by an Indian man who stutters. I told him about similar attitudes that I had found in Japan and about the Japanese stuttering schools' efforts to combat those attitudes. Then we talked about the work that was being done in the United States with stutterers. He seemed especially interested in the idea of adult stutterers' meeting in groups for mutual encouragement and help and in the mechanical aids that I demonstrated for him, particularly the prolongation. When I left him, I said that both Dr. Johnson and I would send him further information about methods of controlling stuttering and material about the philosophy of the Iowa clinic as well.

I flew from Calcutta to Madras, then to Ceylon, and then to Colombo, where I rejoined the *Schwabenstein*. We sailed through the Red Sea and the Suez Canal to Genoa. There I disembarked on January 11, 1955. I had previously arranged to buy a Volkswagen car and to pick it up at that port. In my new Volkswagen, I drove to Barcelona, took a ferry to the island of Majorca, and then drove to the Hotel Bendinat, a hotel that had been recommended by a friend on the *Schwabenstein*. I fell in love with the hotel, and, indeed, with Majorca, and have made several visits to the island since. During the seven weeks that I stayed there my school Spanish improved, although I continued to stutter much more in Spanish than I did in English. Using the Spanish telephones was especially difficult, partly because calls are harder to put through in Spain than they are in the United States—a great deal of explaining to the operator is involved.

In mid-March I left with the car for the south of Spain. After sightseeing for a month, I arrived in Madrid in mid-April. I visited my first European speech school there.

At the Escuela de Ortofonia in Madrid, the sole technique used in the treatment of stutterers was that of speaking in time to a metronome beat. This was basically the Columbat method, which had been developed in the first half of the nineteenth century in France. Before the students put on a little program for me, the head of the stuttering program, Señora Juana de Santos, built up their confidence by giving them a pep talk which sounded like that of a coach before a football game. Then, each student stood up by his seat and spoke to me in time to a beating metronome. Under the influence of the machine, their fluency was very good, although the speech did sound like the tick-tock of a cuckoo clock.

After the speeches, the teacher turned off the metronome and told one of the girls, who was about fourteen, to stand up and speak without it. She stood up and burst into tears. This angered Señora de Santos, who promptly gave the girl a scolding in front of the class. I sat there, embarrassed, but even more distressed at the spectacle of a youngster caught in a rigid therapy program that was not right for her. My heart has gone out to many other stutterers at other times, but never quite so much as it did that day to that girl.

We have known for a long time that the speech of most stutterers will improve when the stutterers are forced, either by deliberate chanting or by some kind of regular mechanical signals, to speak in evenly spaced syllables. Modern electronics has made possible the development of a metronome so small it can be placed, like a hearing aid, behind a stutterer's ear. Only the stutterer can hear the metronome's beat. The use of such a device has recently been part of the stuttering therapy program headed by Dr. David Burns at the University of Pennsylvania. The chief drawback to this treatment arises from the fact that normal speech is full of irregularly timed syllables. Most stutterers will not use metronomic speech in public because of its abnormal sound.

From Madrid I drove into northern Spain, and over the Pyrenees into France. In 1944, when I was nineteen, I had heard Mrs. Gifford speak of the shrine at the French town of Lourdes, and of the miraculous cures that handicapped people had experienced there. In a very positive way she had said that miracles do happen. Since I was near Lourdes anyway, I decided to see for myself what it was like.

After the drive over the Pyrenees in springtime, when everything had been beautifully fresh with lilacs and other flowers in bloom, the actual approach to the town of Lourdes was depressingly commercial. The highway was lined with advertisements, and the town itself seemed to be full of hotels. I signed into one of them, then went to see the shrine.

There was a church with a long park before it. Along the sidewalks and paths that led up to the church I saw people who were ill, in wheelchairs or on portable beds. Many of them were attended by nurses. Someone told me there would be a candlelight march that night. I went back to the hotel.

After dinner I returned to the church and walked up to stand in a group of people near its main door. From there I looked down upon the area of paths and lawns. It was a night on which the moon was almost full. There were small broken clouds moving over the moon, momentarily obscuring its brightness. In the distance I began to hear singing. Slowly there came toward us a long line of marchers, many praying for the recovery of others, some ill themselves but able to walk, some pushed along in wheelchairs. Most of them held lighted candles.

They came nearer, the line serpentine, the beautiful scene partially lit by the moon, with the clouds making passing shadows. The music they were singing was the Lourdes version of the "Ave Maria," and, even now, when I hear it, it stirs up in me the awareness that I had that night of an extraordinary inner stillness and something entering from the world beyond, as though I were in the presence of the Eternal.

It was a rare experience. Whatever it was I felt there made me sure that there is another world beyond the little that we can see. Looking at speech and trying to explain how it works seemed to be comparable to dealing with the leaves of one tree which is part of a forest that is part of a country that is part of a continent. When I hear that there are cures that do occur, documented medical statements of cures at Lourdes of people who were given up as hopeless, I think we are not meant to know how these things happen. We have to take a part of life as unexplainable and try not to question it.

A few weeks later I arrived in Zurich, at the clinic of Dr. Richard Lüchsinger, a well-known speech pathologist. I had written to him earlier, saying that I was a therapist and a stutterer, and that I would like to visit the clinic and observe his therapy methods.

When I got there, I was surprised to find I had been enrolled as a patient. I thought I might as well go ahead and see what I could learn from what was to be my last formal therapy. It was rather general—suggestions about diet, such as cutting down on salt, and counseling regarding the leading of a relatively calm life, trying to look at things as positively as possible. There was some emphasis on trying to develop a more melodic way of speaking. Dr. Lüchsinger's main mechanical therapy was the use of ear plugs, called *sans son*, which kept a stutterer from hearing his own voice. Later, I was to do my Ph.D. dissertation on a related procedure in which stutterers were prevented by the use of a masking noise from hearing themselves speaking.

Stutterers often speak better when they cannot hear their own voices. This discovery has been a by-product of research concerned with the possibility that stuttering might be the result of a hearing disfunction. While the discovery is interesting—it is always tantalizing to find conditions under which the speech of most stutterers consistently improves—its usefulness is greater in the area of research than it is for therapy. The same might be said of metronomic speech. No stutterer who can only speak well when he is wearing a set of headphones or a ticking timepiece will be content with his lot for very long.

In Rome I visited a speech clinic where children who stuttered were taught to paint and speak at the same time. They spoke in time to the movements of their brushes. The therapy was intended to improve rhythmic coordination and at the same time to distract the children, to relax their tension about their speech.

In Vienna the public school speech therapists were using relaxation, measured slow speech, and breathing exercises with young stutterers.

In a Munich clinic I heard an authority say that the most important goal for a stutterer should be to develop speech that was enthusiastic and full of melody and intonation. Instead of working at controlling stuttering, the therapists in this clinic worked as they would with normal speakers on general speech improvement, hoping that the good speech habits—rhythm, projection, and extended voice range—would break through and overpower the stuttering. Along with speech classes, this clinic held general physical activity classes in which the patients did limbering exercises, bending over, arms swinging loosely, and so forth. I enjoyed the unusually warm and relaxed atmosphere in this clinic.

When I got to Copenhagen, I telephoned Dr. Svend Smith, who worked in a school at nearby Hellerup. "Hello," I said, "this is Fred Murray from the United States."

"Hello," he replied, "you are a stut-ter-er, aren't you!" I hadn't actually stuttered, but he had picked it up anyway. He said to come out and see his clinic—he would hang a black cloth out of his office window so I would know in which room I could find him. I went out, looked for the black cloth, and there he was.

Dr. Smith was engaged in an effort to relax stutterers, to get them to ventilate their feelings freely, and to help them reach the instinctive rhythmic levels of oral expression that underlie all acquired speech. In his office I saw drums of many colors, sizes, and designs. His patients would beat on the drums with their hands, while, at the same time, they would dance with spontaneous, natural movements around the room and speak loosely in time to the drumbeats. There was nothing metronomic or organized about the relationship between the drumbeats and the words. A patient might beat: "Be-baAbe-bo-boom—I'm beginning to enjoy this—Boom-de-boom—How are you?—Ba-boom—I'm fine—Boom-de-boom." Since stuttering is not only a matter of being stuck on a sound but also an interruption of the rhythm that underlies the act of speaking, Dr. Smith believed that there was strengthening value in a therapy that helped stutterers find and reinforce the primitive levels of rhythm in their speech. I tried it myself and I must say that I felt quite free afterward.

In Sweden I visited a clinic in which stutterers were treated with tranquilizers. As the Japanese experiments which I had observed the preceding year had shown, and, as most subsequent experiments concerning the effects of tranquilizers on stutterers have also shown, the finding here was that when stuttering is reduced by the use of tranquilizing drugs it seems to be reduced in severity but not in frequency.

The research that has been done in this area has been spotty, and the follow-ups have in general been short ones. At this point we have no firm conclusions to offer the stutterer in regard to drug therapy. If the cause of stuttering can be established, we may someday be able to develop a drug that will help the system stabilize at the time the disorder is developing, and that will prevent the disorder from becoming entrenched.

When I got to Oslo, I was met by a new stepbrother, the son of my father's new wife. He was a little older than I. He had lived in both Norway and the United States, and he spoke the languages of both countries very well. I was lucky to have him with me to translate when we visited a stutterers' school on a farm about eighty miles from Oslo. Stutterers came to board and to receive therapy for several months at a time at this school. It was a lovely place, surrounded by meadows. Both the physical situation and the therapy there reminded me of the program that Dr. Van Riper was running in Michigan. The work was directed toward modifying the behavior of the stutterers so that they would learn to stutter more fluently, with less interruption. They learned to identify their own symptoms, to play with them and to vary them until they could establish new and more useful responses to the cues that usually set off their stuttering. Their aim then was to make those new responses habitual, with a streamlining of their speech the result. As we left, the head of the school said to us that a large part of his method was based on the writings of Dr. Van Riper in the United States.

When I first reached London in September of 1955, I called the College of Speech Therapists, the organization there that is responsible for the training of therapists. Its secretary made arrangements for me to visit several hospital speech clinics. Of the five clinics I visited in London, I was most discouraged by my experience with a therapist who I watched work with a fourteen-year-old boy at St. Paul's Hospital. The boy seemed rather shy as he came into her office, and I soon learned that he stuttered badly. She looked sharply at him and asked, "Well, are you stuttering today, Bobby?"

He said y-y-y-yes he was. She opened up a fairly easy book and had him sit down and read it. He read slowly, but moderately well. However, if he hesitated the slightest bit, she would stop him and make him do that part over. Even if I hadn't seen her glancing at the clock, I would have felt that this was a hurried session. There was nothing calm about her manner, and I believe the boy picked up some of her tension, for he read less and less well as the minutes went by. When his half hour was up, she abruptly dismissed him without any explanation of what that reading was supposed to do to help him.

Much speech therapy is conducted in this nonexplaining way, on the spot, without reference to what will happen in the future or to what has gone on before. It always pays to tell a person who is receiving therapy the reason for assignments, to take advantage of the motivation that invariably appears as he understands that when this little gain is achieved he's going to be standing on the next rung of the ladder.

My favorite visit in England was to the Middlesex Hospital clinic which was run by a therapist named Amy Swallow. She was a short, rather masculine-looking woman, in a white smock, with a pencil stuck through her hair. I liked her very much. She took me up some stairs into a large room that had been curtained off into small compartments, each about eight by ten feet. I could hear what was going on in the compartments around me as I sat watching Miss Swallow work.

In England, the word "stammering" is used for what we call "stuttering" in the United States. Miss Swallow's chief advice, which she drilled into the minds of all who came to her for help was "make friends with your stammer." By this she did not mean either surrender or join the enemy since you'd found you couldn't beat him. She said she meant that the handicap could be tamed. At the time I first heard this I did not understand it nearly so well as I was to understand it later. Years afterward, when I heard Dr. Bluemel say that one of the most valuable things he had learned in his struggle with his own stuttering was to be kind to himself, I remembered Miss Swallow.

Relaxation was another major part of Miss Swallow's therapy. She would teach her patients how to relax, and they would talk to her about the things that bothered them. I watched her with one man who had been in the service. She tried to slow him down; her whole mood changed when she talked to him, and he was able to pattern—to copy her slow, easy way of speaking. She was a warm person who showed concern for her patients. In spite of her no-nonsense attitude, she was very popular with them, and I think she was often successful in her work.

After visiting England, I returned to the United States, landing in New York on the *Queen Elizabeth* and driving across the country to California. On the way I stopped to see friends at a number of speech centers, including Dr. Van Riper at Kalamazoo and Dr. Johnson at Iowa City. I had already written to Dr. Johnson about the stutterer from Calcutta, but, while I was in Iowa City, he and I talked a bit more about what we should send to that anxious man.

During my long drive, I began to construct for myself an overview of the therapies I had seen. None of them seemed perfect to me in that none provided a dependable "cure." However, the therapies that were concerned with stutterers' feelings and their deeply entrenched patterns of tension and struggle seemed to me far more likely to result in solid improvement than the ones involving rigid techniques aimed at the immediate suppression of stuttering.

Those conclusions are ones that I was able to draw at the time of my trip's end, and I agree with them today. As I continued to study, I understood more of the rationales behind the treatments I had seen, as well as more complicated reasons for those treatments' results. With the exception of the three or four commentaries that I have included in the body of this chapter, I am going to postpone further discussion regarding the value of various stuttering therapies until Chapter 23.

The trip was an important experience for me to have at that time. I came back from it impressed with the world-wide existence of the problem, and with the variety of the therapy approaches I had seen. Witnessing all those different therapies in action made me realize more clearly than anything I had read, or heard in college classrooms, what a vast amount we still do not know about the cause of and treatment for stuttering.

Dr. Johnson, in his enlightening book *Because I Stutter*, wrote that he, in writing the book, did not want to risk adding to the reams of nonsense that already had been written about stuttering. It was chiefly through the investigations made on this trip, combined with my own therapeutic experiences, that I learned better to distinguish the nonsensical from the meaningful.

"Queen Mary" sails from Southampton, September 15, 1955. The author sees her off.

20

The First ASHA Speech

In the spring of 1956, school administrators from all over California came to USC to interview prospective teachers at an employment center set up by the university. I put my name on the list, hoping I could find a job in San Diego, which was near the town where my father and stepmother were living, and which has always been one of my favorite cities. There was an opening in San Diego. I filled out an application for it and went through an interview, but then weeks went by and I heard nothing.

In the meantime the Jefferson Union School District of Santa Clara offered me a job working with mentally retarded children. The interviewer, a principal of one of the district schools, was a stutterer, a fact which had made my interview with him go especially well—I felt less nervous than I had in other interviews because I was not alone in the role of stutterer.

I held off, hoping for San Diego, as long as I dared. The day after I accepted the Jefferson post, an offer to do speech therapy in San Diego arrived. I was extremely disappointed, but I had signed the other contract, so off I went to Santa Clara.

Although I was not enthusiastic about the job, I was looking forward to one aspect of my new situation—the prospect of living with my good friend, Mel Hoffman, whom I had known since we met in one of the evening stutterers' groups at Stanford. Mel had landed a job near mine, so we found a third roommate and rented a house in nearby Palo Alto.

The principal of my school thought that my background qualified me to work with mentally retarded youngsters, as well as those with speech and hearing problems. He gave me a class of fifteen, whose ages ranged from eleven to sixteen and whose average IQ was fifty. It wasn't long before I knew I was in for a rough year. I had studied the needs of retarded children, but I had never actually worked with them, and I did not know how to keep this class from getting out of hand. They would ignore my directions, think up troublesome pranks such as boiling up wax crayons in the pots on our electric hot plate, and become violent, throwing large wooden blocks and other objects around the room.

The teachers in the neighboring rooms, hearing the pandemonium, would send for the principal. All of a sudden the door to my room would open, and there he would be standing with a very firm look on his face. Each student would freeze in the middle of whatever he was doing, there would be silence for a minute or so, and then the students would begin to pick up the mess.

I asked the advice of administrators and of teachers, and I read books and articles on the handling of children such as these, but, perhaps because I had so thoroughly lost it, I could not maintain control. The outbreaks got worse and worse. I was tired and unhappy, and my speech deteriorated along with my spirits. One day one of the boys looked at me and said, "Mr. Murray, you talk crooked." The description was accurate. In fact, I dare say that it describes stuttering behavior more accurately than many professional terms.

Early that fall I had been invited to speak about stuttering therapy in Japan as part of a program that was being organized for the November ASHA national convention to be held in Chicago. I was thrilled to be asked to do this, but I was not sure I was up to it. The preceding summer I had spoken without much trouble about my trip at a Western Speech Association meeting in Oregon, but that had been a small group, and in the background there had been a slight but continuous sound of clatter from an adjoining kitchen that made me feel less nervous. Speaking at the annual convention of the national organization would be a different matter.

However, the invitation was more than just flattering—it was a chance to help my career along. I asked my superintendent for permission to be away from school for the speech, received it, and sent off my acceptance to the ASHA program committee.

That very day I began having abnormal amounts of anxiety, as though on my radar I had picked up signals of a devastating storm that would not hit for weeks. Thus, I wrote a letter to Dr. Johnson expressing my fears. He answered cheerfully that if he, who had once stuttered many times worse than I ever had, could get through ASHA convention speeches, I shouldn't have much to worry about. Nevertheless, compulsive dread regarding the speech filled my mind much of the time. When the day finally came for me to leave, before I went to the plane I told Mel that I might telephone him from Chicago and ask him to play on our phonograph a certain march that usually made me feel strong and confident. He said that he would do that, but he was sure I wouldn't need it. I wasn't so sure.

The speech, one of several on different topics that were being given by members of a panel, was scheduled for mid-morning the next day. I went through my usual pre-emergency spasms of pain, except that this time they were as bad or worse than any I had ever suffered before. This wasn't going to be an empty junior high school auditorium, it was going to be an eight hundred seat hall filled with members of the most sophisticated speech organization in the world.

Joseph Sheehan was the coordinator of the panel. When I walked into the hall, I saw him up on the stage, making sure everything was set at the podium. The audience began to file in. I climbed the steps to the stage and sat in the seat assigned me, knowing that I was going to be called on for the third spot.

As the program began and the first speaker went to the podium, I began to experience a visual, almost a spatial, sense of disorientation, similar to the one I had suffered back in 1940. When my turn came and I reached the podium, I opened my mouth and went immediately into tremors, the first I had had in eleven years. I had almost no control. Besides the tremors, I was battling severe blockages that I could not seem to pull out of. The more I tried to prevent their happening, the worse they were. Somehow I struggled on, even though the ghastly tremors and the blocking continued. At last I blurted out the final word and sat down, burning with shame.

It was a stinging defeat for me, one that colored my reactions for weeks afterward. I had been enormously proud of my invitation to speak at this meeting, and, while I'd known I would probably have some difficulty, I never dreamed I would totally fall apart. Nowdays, I refer to this as the "Hindenburg Speech," named for the German dirigible that exploded in New Jersey in 1937.

The next day I flew back to California, back to the mentally retarded class, where no matter how I tried, nothing improved. In March the superintendent sent me a letter saying that I was evidently working in the wrong field, and that he would like me to move over into speech therapy the following week. The two speech therapists who were already in that school made room for me. It was very nice of them. After I had been on the new job a week or two, my friends began to tell me how much better I looked. Well, I guess I did.

■ ── ■

I met Dr. Bryngelson for the first time as I was leaving the hall after my catastrophic ASHA speech. He said, "Young man, you exemplified today everything that I say about stuttering. Your behavior was further proof for me that stuttering is neurologically determined. What you were going through was a neurological disintegration, typical of what I have said can happen to severe stutterers.

"What you should have done was to start your speech by saying that you are a stutterer, and then you should have gone ahead and have done some voluntary stuttering, bouncing and so forth. Instead, you were trying to fight it, to hide it."

How right this wise, scientific clinician was. He helped to wash the windows of my mind. How much I came to learn from him in ensuing years! In Chicago, as I had in Stockton five years earlier, I wanted to keep from stuttering altogether. I hoped that my everyday fluency would somehow, magically, be able to stand up against the strain of the situation. I was trying to wish myself into being the Fred Murray that I thought I would ultimately be, that I never have become. The role demand was totally unrealistic.

■ ——————————————————————————————— ■

Today, I would go into a speech like that one with a much more relaxed and open mind. I am sure that if I started to stutter now the way I did there I could at least turn and guide my mechanism so that it would do other things, so that my words would flow better. I was not able to do that on the 1956 occasion mainly because of my terror. There is a point on the fear or pressure scale beyond which no technique, either psychological or mechanical, can prevent a person's stuttering.

Since 1956 I have learned that there are alternative plans, like safety nets, that I can build into any situation. If plan number one does not work, I can resort, or drop down, to number two. And if that fails, I can fall to number three and still survive. This hierarchy of safety nets can be divided into two parts: the psychological—the way a person feels and the way he looks at himself in a situation, and the physical—the way he handles his speech mechanism. This alternative plans idea helped make my 1965 speech at ASHA quite successful and my 1977 ASHA speech to five hundred people even more so.

On the top level a person does not try to exercise any psychological or physical control. He just goes into the situation and starts to talk, leaving his speech mechanism to handle itself automatically. If he finds he is having difficulty, he can move to the second level and, as Dr. Bryngelson suggested, announce that he is a stutterer. Physically, again as Dr. Bryngelson suggested, he can begin to do some extra stuttering. He might make a statement such as "I'd like first of all to declare that I am a stutterer, and that I'm having some difficulty. I'm a bit nervous here, and I'd like to make myself stutter a little more than I actually have to." Then, as he gives the speech, putting in deliberate slides occasionally to give himself leeway to breathe, he will be establishing himself in both word and action in the role of stutterer, thereby relaxing the demand that he feels from that situation.

Then, on level number three, if the declaration and the deliberate stuttering have not been sufficient and he feels a panic coming, if he is really jamming up, he can probably k-k-k-k-keep the mechanism going with strong vo-vo-vo-voluntary movements and work it through that way. If he should still bungle it, he should go back at the end, making no apology, and say something like the following: "Well, this has been one hell of an experience. I've stuttered continually. Nothing that I tried seemed to work. But I'm going to try to salvage something out of it, and here's what I think I'll try to do next time. . . ." At the very least he will have the satisfaction of having ended on an objective note, of having gained something from the experience, and of having held onto a degree of control, even through the failure.

Today, knowing that I have the security of nets two and three under me, that I have alternatives, I find that I stay on level one most of the time, even in very stressful situations.

∎ ———————————————————————————————— ∎

The appearance of tremors in my speech after eleven years without them is undoubtedly an example of what the late Dr. George Kopp of Wayne State University would call a psychomotor pattern reactivated by stress. Dr. Kopp believed that speech patterns of all kinds are recorded in the neurological pathways of the brain, like tracks on phonograph records that can be replayed. We know that the brain develops outward from the center, with the newer development toward the surface. When a child stutters, imprints are made in his brain. If, later, his speech improves, that improvement will also be imprinted in subsequent outer brain layers.

At any one point during the rest of his life his speech under relaxed circumstances will probably be directed by his brain's higher or outer layers. But, if there is sudden stress, shaking up his organism to the point where deeper brain levels are reactivated, whatever is stored deep down in the brain may come forth and be expressed in behavior. We know that the cerebral cortex, the top part of the brain, monitors voluntary behavior; however, under sudden emotion or stress, the cortex is somewhat inhibited, allowing deeply stored patterns to surface.

Several years ago I saw a Baltimore psychiatrist who was a stutterer stand up to address an ASHA convention. He had been through twelve years of therapy, and I knew that his ordinary speech was very good. As he came up to the microphone, his face suddenly took on an expression that could have belonged to a man standing in a tub full of water with his finger in an electric socket. His face twisted into wild grimaces and spasms. He was trying to start his speech, but he was making no sound. This went on for almost one minute. Finally, he was able to stop the contortions. He took a little pause, and then he went into his speech and spoke quite well. Afterwards, he told me that years earlier his stuttering had consisted in part of that grimacing behavior. Under the strain of having to address the seven hundred people in that room, he had momentarily reverted to one of his old patterns.

Dr. Kopp's theory that nothing learned is ever forgotten is reinforced, I believe, by experiments that have been conducted with hypnosis. A typical one involved a man of sixty who had come to the United States from Spain when he was nine years old. He learned to speak English in the United States, and, by the time he was fourteen, he was fluent in his new language. He did not speak Spanish for more than forty years, and his speech had no trace of a Spanish accent. When asked to speak Spanish, he said he had forgotten everything. Nevertheless, under deep hypnosis, which took him back to age seven, he spoke in fluent Spanish. Apparently, the hypnosis was able to bypass the higher centers of the brain.

Hypnosis has also been used in connection with stuttering. One type of hypnosis is suggestive in nature and tries to eliminate tension and fear of speaking. Another, explorative in nature, attempts to unearth the cause of stuttering. Many stutterers have erroneously presumed that if the cause were to be found their stuttering would cease. This is similar to thinking that a fire that is consuming a house will extinguish itself merely because the match that started it has been found in an adjacent field.

I often use an analogy which deals with hypnosis and stuttering in my lectures. To travel from City A to City B is a distance of a thousand miles. One can fly there in a comfortable jet plane in two hours. Or, one can get there via a horseback trail through mountainous terrain. The trail is rough, often muddy, containing elements of a disease that is rampant in City B. The person who travels by jet will probably not be exposed to the disease; or, if he is, he will not have sufficient time to build a resistance against it. On the other hand, the person who travels by trail, a journey of several weeks, will have time to develop some immunity and, in all likelihood, will be able to stay in City B without falling helpless victim to the disease that is on the rampage there.

Hypnosis for stuttering is similar to the plane ride. It momentarily separates the individual from the interactive forces of life—the pressures and strains of reality. However, it does not provide the necessary ingredients to deal with these inevitable cues, once they again must be faced and dealt with.

■ ————————————————————————————————— ■

Back in California after the Chicago speech, I resumed my usual life routines—first, struggling with the unruly class, and then being over-joyed by being transferred into work that I knew how to do. I went on living with my two friends, doing my share of the domestic chores and enjoying their company, just as I had done before.

However, something had changed. The defeat in Chicago had been more than one isolated humiliation. It seemed to have lifetime signifi-cance for me. Involved in that significance were the European therapies I had seen, my analysis, my experiences at The University of Iowa summer program, moments from my childhood, and most of the events of my life that had to do with my stuttering. Although I could not yet identify this significance, I felt that some kind of almost evolutionary change was going on inside me and that, since my preoccupation with what had happened in Chicago and with my old experiences did not seem to be lessening, it might not be long before I would understand consciously what was going on in the deeper levels of my mind.

21

Acceptance

Many stutterers have laughed at a story about two men who meet on a train. The first asks the second where he is going.

The second replies, "D-D-D-D-Detroit."

"Wh-Wh-Wh-Wh-Wh-What for?"

"T-T-T-T-T-T-T-To see Dr. Smith."

'D-D-D-D-D-Dr. Smith! The sp-sp-sp-sp-sp-sp-speech therapist?"

"Wh-Wh-Wh-Wh-Wh-why, yes. Do you no-no-no-no-no-no-no-know him?"

"Know him? He cu-cu-cu-cu-cu-cu-cu-cured me!"

They laugh, but there is a bittersweet quality to their laughter because every stutterer has hoped for a cure, and most have thought at some time they have found one. The symptom is so volatile, so susceptible to suggestion, that the substantial improvement which often comes quickly at the start of a new therapy frequently appears to be a sign that at last the cure has been found. But, then, the stutterer finds that his improvement is only temporary. As Dr. Sheehan said in the ASHA "Recovered" Stutterers' Panel of 1968, "One of the troubles with being a stutterer is that nearly everything that anybody suggests will work temporarily, and nothing that anybody suggests will work permanently."

One explanation for the temporary success of many therapies involves the role change that a stutterer undergoes when he moves into a therapy situation. He turns into the special person who has come to be helped, and everything around him is cooperating to make that expectation come true. The luxury during therapy of being able to concentrate entirely on one's speech further increases that therapy's chances of being momentarily effective. In many stuttering therapies the teaching of physical and mental relaxation is important, and relaxation, as Mrs. Gifford knew so well, is always conducive to fluency. Furthermore, the isolated and protected nature of almost every therapy situation encourages a kind of relaxation which is characterized by diminishing fear. This is probably the major reason why the proponents of so many stuttering therapies can point to a fast initial decrease in stuttering—stuttering is dramatically increased by fear.

Dr. West made a useful distinction between what he called the "symptom" and the "syndrome" of stuttering. The "symptom" is what we see and hear in the way of stuttering behavior. The "syndrome" is what is underneath, all the things that are responsible for the stuttering's occurring. Affecting the syndrome are the complicated psychological forces that are operating to perpetuate the handicap, such as the person's conditioned fears, or cues. The psychomotor stuttering patterns that are imprinted in successive levels of the brain's cortex are part of the stuttering syndrome. So are some deeply rooted physical behavior patterns involving the speech mechanism.

While the stuttering symptom may fluctuate dramatically in both severity and duration in response to the stutterer's surroundings and his expectations, the syndrome is relatively stable. Changes in the syndrome, such as a response to the aggravation or a reduction of a habitual fear tied to stuttering, occur more slowly. Stuttering's "instant cures" become manifest on the symptom level. The reason they do not last is that the syndrome remains largely unaffected.

■ ———————————————————————————————————— ■

By 1956 I had heard many of the stuttering specialists say that they did not believe an adult stutterer could rid himself of his problem completely. Back in Iowa I had heard Dr. Johnson say that he knew of no way that the adult could get away from all the problems involved in stuttering. On another occasion I heard him refer to "the days when I thought I knew how to cure stuttering."

I had read an article published in a 1939 *Journal of Speech Disorders* in which Dr. Kopp had written: "No one has ever cured an adult stutterer."

I knew that Dr. Bryngelson was famous for saying: "Once a stutterer, always a stutterer."

And I had also watched the officers of ASHA fuss over quotation marks around the word, "'Recovered,'" so that no one attending the Stutterers' Panels would think that either the association or the panel members thought of the panel members as permanently cured.

I suppose as far back as my summer at Iowa I began in some remote part of myself to acknowledge that my speech difference was a permanent one, but I resisted that recognition. I continued to dream of a cure and to hide my stuttering at any cost. As late as the spring before my Chicago speech, when I was thirty years old, I refused to read a story to a group of first grade children at USC because I was afraid I would stutter and that they would laugh at me.

But, after the Chicago experience, I no longer believed I could will my way to fluency. It was partly the surfacing of my old tremors that made me finally appreciate and accept the irradicable and deeply complex nature of my disability, of the syndrome beneath the symptom. I said to myself: "This thing has been with you a long time, almost all your life. You are never going to find that golden answer that you thought was possible when you were a child."

■ ─── ■

I was at last accepting the self-concept of stutterer, the step that the Iowa clinicians had said was preliminary to successful therapy. In a way I had been beaten down to it by many earlier experiences, most recently by my search through Europe for an ideal therapy and by my humiliation at the ASHA convention.

But, because the apparent defeat was actually a step forward, I didn't feel beaten down. I felt relieved. And soon I began to reap some benefits. Although I had not been willing to receive it wholeheartedly, most of what I had learned at Iowa was still available to me in my memory, standing by ready to be used. I recalled some of the assignments we had been given there in which we were supposed to show outsiders that we were stutterers. Throwing away my earlier aversion to such exercises, for the first time I voluntarily stuttered in front of strangers without shame.

As I shed my false pride about fluency, I began, gladly, to shed as well the feelings of guilt about stuttering that had clung to me for so long. My defensive feelings about stuttering also began slowly to fade away.

As I reduced my avoiding, I reduced the strain of pretending to be someone I was not. I dropped the guard I had been holding up for nearly thirty years, and with that came further relaxation and a surge of spontaneity and surprising joy.

Best of all, with the acceptance of myself as a stutterer, I was able to complete a growth process that I had partly accomplished during my analysis, a process that Dr. Sheehan has called the "integration of role." This was the acceptance of my total self, not just the fluent me. I found that I liked myself more than I had before.

Everyone, stutterer or not, must achieve this total acceptance if he is to live peacefully. I suppose for some stutterers, those who have been brought up in exceptionally loving, understanding atmospheres and who have been taught not to be afraid of what is real, it may even be easy to do. With my background and personality, it was extremely hard for me to accept my stuttering. I am not ashamed of having come to it so late—I believe the person I was could not have achieved that surrender without a long struggle. What matters is that I did achieve it, and it turned my life around.

As the months went by, my emotions of relief were replaced by something stronger. All my life I had looked forward to my victory over stuttering—to the achievement of normal speech. But now I saw that the true victory lay in acknowledging and accepting my stuttering, in becoming, in Miss Swallow's words, its "friend."

■ ─── ■

Along with my other gains, I had a new surge of energy at this time, and I wanted to take advantage of it. I felt an urge to begin some kind of constructive program that would help me in my career. As I reevaluated my speech with the aim of setting up realistic, attainable goals, I decided that I should work on speaking before an audience. I had done very little of it, and I was afraid of it; but if I were going to be a teacher, I had to learn to do it easily.

I thought the matter over, wondering if I could try to find an audience that wouldn't care much whether I stuttered a lot, mildly, or not at all. It occurred to me that near San José there was a rather famous mental institution. I went to see the person in charge of volunteers there, told her that I had some slides of my travels in Europe and Asia, and asked if some of the patients might like to see a slide show. She invited me to give a trial talk, and my career as a lecturer began.

At first I was very nervous, but I was getting a chance to speak before a group, and it felt good to be doing something to help myself. There were about sixty in those audiences. Although I suppose about half weren't paying much attention to what I was saying, many of the patients seemed to enjoy it, stuttering or not. Sometimes I would hear sudden laughter when I hadn't said anything funny, and every so often a patient would go out of control and would have to be carried out of the room; nevertheless, I kept on showing slides and talking, hammering away, and, as time went by, I began to feel more confident and to speak more fluently. Although I was helped in this project by assuming the role of lecturer, I think my major improvement came from what my Iowa clinicians would have called "deconditioning the fear." I got in there and kept performing the feared act until it began to lose some of its frightening aspects.

After the mental hospital slide shows ended, I gave myself another push. I looked into the San José adult education program and was hired to give a series of weekly travel lectures, beginning in October and ending in May. I did this for two years. One week the talk might be on France, another on Spain, and so forth. The audiences ranged in number from forty to ninety. I stuttered, of course, but I got much better with practice, and soon I found I was enjoying myself. The mental hospital had provided the means to get momentum; once I had that momentum, I transferred it to something a little harder, something a little closer to my teaching goal.

■ ——————————————————————————————————— ■

I wish I had known enough during my high school days to have made this kind of effort. Being active helps to keep down the dreadful anxieties that preoccupy many stutterers' thinking. The feeling of having a forward-moving campaign, getting the ratio of the positive speech experiences to exceed the negative, is marvelous indeed.

Severe stutterers particularly need to find situations similar to my mental hospital one, situations in which they are likely to experience success, no matter what the conditions are. Then they can use those successes as steppingstones from which they can move gradually toward greater challenges. Stutterers should not attempt to do something that is more than they can possibly handle; however, they often can discover projects in which they are bound to succeed more often than they will fail.

■ ——————————————————————————————————— ■

Shortly after I began the mental hospital slide shows, I began to work on my telephone anxieties in a direct way. The cues that I had accumulated over the years were formidable, but I started in anyway to do what I could to decondition those fears. I did not permit myself to dodge any telephoning tasks that came up in my work or in my private life; in fact, I began actively to look for reasons to make phone calls.

At first it was so difficult I could not imagine improvement, but gradually I began to perceive slight signs of change. As I kept at this deconditioning process during the succeeding months and, finally, years, the act of telephoning slowly lost its terrifying character and became merely upsetting; then what had been upsetting became merely difficult. But, I could only make that happen by putting my hand on the instrument and dialing calls, over and over. After years of trying, I finally got the fear down in that way. I think it was Robert Frost who once said, "The best way out is through."

■ ——————————————————————————————————— ■

Since the problem once appeared almost insurmountable, it is not surprising that today I occasionally have moments in which I feel some anxiety about making a call. Such leftover reactions, or residuals, pop up to surprise the most improved stutterer from time to time, often in response to an old cue, or when he is tired or ill. Stutterers soon learn that the appearance of one of these reactions is not a sign of impending relapse. These reactions are like body memories, slight twinges that are sometimes felt in the physical body in areas of old injury, long after healing has occurred. If a person has established himself in his own mind as a stutterer, he will not have to feel defensive when these inescapable residuals sporadically appear.

■ ─── ■

In my work as a speech therapist I had many opportunities to demonstrate my new attitude toward my stuttering. Besides working with students and with the other therapists, I was frequently involved in conferences with teachers, school administrators, parents, and people from the community. Phone calls were necessary to make arrangements for most of these meetings. At the meetings I often had to introduce strangers to each other—another chance to face old demons as a declared stutterer and, without avoiding, to work each problem through. At the start, these introductions were every bit as tough for me as the phone calls were. Sometimes I felt as though I were standing in back of myself to keep myself from running away. I am glad to say that the introductions, too, have become considerably easier through the years.

■ ─── ■

Besides the many meetings that were held at school, as part of my speech therapy work, I was required to make visits to the homes of my students, to talk to their parents, and to get an idea of the atmosphere in which each youngster lived. These home visits had been required of public school speech therapists back when I was in elementary school. In theory they are an important part of the therapy, since the therapists should be able to help parents modify their home environment in ways that will relieve unnecessary pressures on their child.

Practically, however, these visits often do not accomplish nearly as much as they should. One reason is that therapists usually do not have nearly enough time to spend on home visits. Often they can make only a few relatively short visits each year to an individual child's home. Sometimes a couple of visits per year is all that time will allow.

These days, with both parents working in more and more families, therapists often find that no one is at home during the school hours in which visits are usually made. In families where both parents are working there is so much to do after work hours that, even if the therapist is able to make evening home calls, relaxed and thoughtful visits are hard to achieve.

And when time is not a problem for either the therapist or the parent, the therapist may still find that a home visit is ineffective because a parent is uncooperative. Defiant expressions of pride, or wishes for privacy that are unreasonable under the circumstances, may be blanketing a parent's refusal to admit even to himself the nature and extent of his child's handicap.

My very first visit, which I made on March 22, 1957, turned out to be my most memorable. The appointment was at the home of a little girl, a severe stutterer, who often arrived at school in tears after a stormy session with her temperamental mother. The child's teachers had learned through painful experience that the mother would take offense at the most circumspect suggestions from the school, and that she was a person who always delivered her complaints in person.

It was an unfortunate choice for my first home visit. As I drove out to that house, I searched my mind for tactful phrases. I was sure I would stutter because I was so nervous, and I was determined to be open about it. It was possible that this woman, whom I had never met, would speak scornfully about my being a stutterer. I took a deep breath as I pressed her doorbell.

The door was opened by a pretty blond woman in a flowered dress whose face bore an expression of madonna calm. She led me into an immaculate living room, where at first I could not think of a way to bring up her little girl's need for peace at home. This room's order was so extreme it was unreal. Equally unreal was the soft voice of the mother as she went on and on about her bewilderment over messages from school concerning her daughter's nervous symptoms. I described the child's frequently hysterical behavior when she first arrived at school, but the mother refused to admit that my accounts could be true. She, herself, was an easy-going person, her daughter was always quiet and content, and nothing ever went on in the home to make her otherwise.

I was obviously wasting everybody's time. I gathered up my papers and started to stand when, all of a sudden, the floor seemed to tilt and almost to knock me back into my chair. One of California's more severe earthquakes was underway. My hostess screamed, said some words I had not heard that day, and started crawling across the rug to the doorway, where she would be safest if the house collapsed. There she huddled, screaming and shouting to me to come and help her. I didn't care if the house did collapse, I would not have joined her in that doorway for anything, so I continued to sit in my chair, waiting for the shaking and the screaming to die down. When the earthquake was over, I found to my dismay that she had decided to blame me for unmasking her calm.

If a small stutterer's teachers, therapist, and parents are cooperating with each other to help him, his chances of reducing and possibly even of eliminating his handicap are as high as they can possibly be. Because of this, every effort to enlist the support of noncooperative parents should be made.

Sometimes there are subtle ways in which families can be educated about the dangers of overprotection. Sometimes more severe methods need to be employed to jolt parents out of excessive self-concern and into active attention to their child's needs. One therapist I knew invited several such parents to spend an evening with a group of severe adult stutterers. Afterwards, those parents all said they would be willing to do anything to help their children avoid that fate.

■ ─────────────────────────────────────── ■

In December, 1961, my father, several friends of mine, and I were staying at the Furnace Creek Ranch in California's Death Valley. Death Valley is one of my favorite spots in the world. It is a place where I feel as though I am far away from everything in my ordinary life, almost on another planet, because the terrain looks something like the moon—a barren, wide, still valley, with beautiful mountains and sand dunes. I love to be there in the winter when the weather is usually clear and mild.

Occasionally guests at the ranch give slide shows, so during my visit I volunteered to show my pictures of South Africa, where I had been the year before. Knowing my father's habits, I asked my friends to bring him into the auditorium just after I had started talking, when the room was dark. "If he's in there early," I said, "he's going to be giving me advice, telling me how to do things such as pull the microphone cord around, and it will make me uneasy."

They did what I asked. I knew when they came in, but I did not look at them or interrupt what I was saying. By then, I was so secure in the role of lecturer that even my father's presence did not disturb me.

That evening is the only time that a member of my family has heard me in a lecture situation. I spoke on South Africa and showed the pictures, and my father heard me. He was very pleased. He told me afterwards that he never thought a person who was in the shape I had been in as a child could end up speaking in public. It meant much to me to hear him say that.

22

Dr. Van Riper

As time passed, I found the label of stutterer to be less and less of a burden. Having made peace with my enemy, I discovered that he was surprisingly responsive to my efforts to manage him. I became my own therapist—my last formal therapy had been back in Dr. Lüchsinger's Swiss clinic. The energy that I had for so long been expending in the struggle against stuttering was suddenly available for me to use in benign control, and it transformed familiar methods and principles, giving them new meanings and new effectiveness.

Once I had dropped my compulsive watching for situations that might make me stutter, I had undistracted attention to give to many different techniques which had been developed by a number of different people. I had come to understand that the habit part of stuttering had to be changed by action, not by thought. However, my brand of stuttering was particularly susceptible to Dr. Van Riper's and Dr. Sheehan's brands of therapy, for it is to their ideas and their writings that I have returned most often throughout my life. In 1957 and 1958, when I first really took hold of my speech difficulties in an integrated way, it was from them that I got most of my help in planning *where* and *how* to go.

As I have already indicated, Dr. Sheehan's therapeutic method, in its briefest form, involves avoidance reduction and integration of role as its main elements.

In order to describe Dr. Van Riper's approach more fully, I must present and comment on his "Suggestions for Stutterers," which I first read in the *Journal of Speech and Hearing Disorders* in the late 1940's. Later, the leader of a therapy group that I joined at USC brought in the suggestions to share with us. One of the many reasons they appeal to me is that they are presented in a kind of therapy ladder, set up in progressive steps. Over the years these suggestions have stood up well, as reminders for the management of my own speech, and as tools to use in my work with other stutterers.

There are fourteen suggestions. The words in italics are Dr. Van Riper's, and the comments that follow are mine.

1. *You must understand the over-all plan of treatment.* In describing a therapy observed in London, I have already written that people usually do better when they know something about the reasons for what they are doing. A stutterer needs to understand, at least in a general way, how he got into the thicket in which he finds himself, and to have a broad idea of the plan that is to be used to help him improve. Explanations prior to therapy are particularly helpful at those moments when the stutterer is asked to do something that is distasteful to him, that kicks off painful emotions from his past, or that makes him stutter badly. Knowing also that this is only one part of the therapy makes a hard phase easier to get through.

2. *You must, for the time being, be willing to stutter openly and without embarrassment.* This point is, obviously, one that I did not appreciate fully until my change of attitude in 1957. In encouraging a person to be open about his stuttering, a therapist is usually opening gates that have been shut for years. Keeping the gates shut and avoiding seems to promise temporary relief, but it always means trouble in the future.

3. *You must acquire the ability to keep good eye contact with your listener throughout your moment of stuttering.* This point has been touched on in my description of the Iowa program. Maintaining eye contact may sound easy. For many people it is very hard. The effort should be started early in therapy. I know stutterers who have gone through various therapies with considerable success, but who still have been unable to break their old habit of looking away from their listener when a block begins. Probably behind it is that the stutterer does not want to see wincing, pained reactions to his blocking behavior.

Everyone knows the feeling of something wrong, of halfway communication, when he is addressed by a person who does not look at him. When a stutterer maintains eye contact with his listener, he is saying, "I am not so ashamed of my stuttering that I cannot look at you."

4. *You must stop avoiding feared words and speech situations.* This is the only suggestion about which I have any reservations. I agree that avoidances must be given up, but I believe they should be reduced gradually, no faster than the stutterer can do so without undue anxiety. Compulsivity to go ahead and make the attempt on every difficult word, or to go into every difficult situation, can only result in an increase in speech breakdowns, in anxiety from repeated failures that outweighs momentary gains.

When a stutterer does begin to use feared words and to go into feared situations, he will be exposing areas of psychic disorder. He must keep participating, trying the feared words repeatedly until he learns that he can put his hand on the stove and not get burned.

5. *You must stop postponements, half-hearted speech attempts, and retrials.* I am postponing if somebody asks me my name and I reply, "My

name is ah, yes, let me see, well, it seems to me, what I mean is my name is Fred Murray."

A *"retrial"* is a postponement device in which the speaker repeats a word or a phrase in an effort to put off saying a difficult word or phrase that is coming. I am resorting to retrials when I say, "My name is, my name, my *name*, yes, my name is Fred Murray."

6. *You must be able to analyze your own stuttering in terms of its varying symptoms.* The stutterer must begin to learn the geography of his speech articulators—to become aware of his lips and the front of his tongue, and to be able to distinguish the points where tension occurs during his blocks. As he becomes familiar with the way his speech mechanism is behaving, he will reach a point where he will be able to describe most of what is happening when he stutters.

7. *You must learn to cancel.* "Cancellation" is a technique in which the stutterer goes right through an old stuttering block, pauses to study what he has just done, and then tries the word again by stuttering in a different, less abnormal, way. It is valuable because it forces a person to correct abnormalities when they occur. If they are left uncorrected, improper speech is reinforced, and future speech is affected adversely.

8. *You must master the principle of negative practice.* By this Dr. Van Riper means that a stutterer must be able to duplicate at will samples of each of his old stuttering patterns. He can do this only if he thoroughly understands what it is he has been doing when he stutters.

9. *You must uncondition or weaken your habitual reactions of approach or release.* "Approach" refers to the way a person goes into the saying of a word, and *"release"* refers to the way he comes out of it. This step is especially important for severe stutterers who have developed complicated approach and release patterns. Often the abnormality is not really in the saying of the feared word, but in the ritual of tense, bizarre behavior which, as an anticipatory reaction to a block, precedes the saying, or in the midst of which the block suddenly ends, and the person can go on to his next word. No matter how strange the behavior, it is reinforced each time it is found to be helpful in starting or ending a word, and eventually that behavior, often accompanied by feelings of humiliation, becomes deeply conditioned. Several abnormal release patterns were described in Chapter 18.

Once a stutterer has deconditioned his habitual approaches to a word, he can prepare to say that word in a more fluent way. He must learn how to keep his speech mechanism in a relaxed state that will permit its being molded for the beginning sound of a feared word. He must learn how to determine the right position, how to get his mechanism into that position, and how, keeping a forward flow of sound, to approach the word directly.

Deconditioning a word's release usually involves voluntary stuttering—changing involuntary, contorted behavior into voluntary behavior (such as using the bounce or the prolongation) in which the block can be terminated with the speaker in control.

10. *You must learn how to pull out of your old blocks voluntarily, to get them under voluntary control before uttering the word.* The last point in step nine is what Dr. Van Riper is referring to in this suggestion.

11. *You must learn how to prepare for the speech attempt of feared words, so that they can be spoken without interruption or abnormality.* Research has shown that most of the time a stutterer has some warning when a bad block is coming. After practicing the techniques involved in steps one to ten, he should be able to turn this warning to good purpose, taking the time between the warning and the moment when he must say the word to relax his speech mechanism and to get it ready to assume the appropriate preparatory set, instead of the habitual, unnatural position that has got him into trouble before.

At first, this substituting of learned behavior when saying feared words will take conscious effort and much voluntary control. However, eventually, it can become so automatic that the stutterer will be able to continue speaking and the substituting will usually occur without his consciously thinking about it.

12. *You must learn how to build barriers against disturbing influences.* To a large extent this important effort will be a personal one. The individual must strive to identify the influences in his life that disturb him, and then he must find ways to deal with them. This will call for a more objective attitude on his part.

Furthermore, many stutterers are troubled by imaginary problems, such as the common tendency to project onto everyone the stutterer meets extreme anti-stuttering reactions that may have been exhibited or expressed by a few listeners in the past. One way to deal with imaginary problems is by doing some of the reality testing which Dr. Johnson advocated. The stutterer can conduct his own opinion polls to find out what is actually going on in a particular situation. In the case of projected opinions, he will undoubtedly discover that the thoughts of his listeners are not half so derogatory as he has thought them to be.

13. *You must learn to fill much of your speech with voluntary loose movements of your tongue, lips, and jaws.* This, of course, involves *"proprioception,"* an awareness of the movements of some of the major parts of the speech mechanism. The more attention one pays to these movements and to the forward flowing of his speech, the more sensitive he will be to their variations, and the better he will be able to guide his mechanism when that becomes necessary.

Even in his free speech it is a good idea for a stutterer occasionally to pay attention to the movement patterns of his mouth, not only because his speech will be better as a result but also because frequent conscious practicing of loose, forward-moving articulation tends to make habitual a kind of speech in which bad blocking rarely occurs.

14. *You must learn how to reinforce your new fluency each day.* For the most part this is accomplished by doing a lot of talking and by using proprioception. Acquiring fluency is one thing. Keeping it is something else. One has to run his own maintenance program.

One other quotation from Dr. Van Riper's writings seems to me to sum up his therapy and its goals. I like it very much—its last three sentences, particularly, are often in my mind.

The quotation may be found in *Stuttering: Significant Theories and Therapies,* Second Edition, by Eugene F. Hahn. At the end of a nine-point list describing the way he deals with the secondary or advanced stutterer, Dr. Van Riper has written:

> 9. *Teach the stutterer how to stutter with a minimum of interruption and abnormality and a maximum of control and insight.*
>
> I think that in the last item lies the most important factor in what success I have had with severe stutterers. It is possible to "stutter" in a great many ways, and I prefer a way which provokes no social penalty or thwarting to communication. By eliminating the habitual symptoms of approach or release we change the form and duration of the speech abnormality. This in itself frees the stutterer from the fears and shame which act as precipitating etiological factors and hence reduces the number of blockings. By teaching the stutterer how to turn involuntary blockings into voluntary ones and how to maintain a voluntary control of the movement sequence in words stuttered upon, we eliminate much of the abulia, hesitation, panic, and confusion. In other words, our immediate aim is, not the prevention of moments of stuttering, but rather the acquisition of skill in controlling the form and duration of the stuttering reactions. Controlled stuttering rather than avoided or prevented stuttering is our objective. If you give a severe stutterer a way of stuttering which causes no social penalty, you prevent relapse and create a fundamental security. Fluent speech and the conquest of the handicap are thereby assured.

■ ——————————————————————————— ■

I stayed on in the Jefferson Schools until June of 1962, with the exception of one year in which I took a leave of absence and went for nine months to Australia to be a therapist and a teacher at the Royal Alexandra Children's Hospital in Sydney. I enjoyed these years very much. It was extremely satisfying to feel my therapeutic skills increasing and to see improvement in cases on which I was working.

And sometimes, less formally, I was able to help my friends. Jim, a close friend of mine from Sydney, was married in 1961. He asked me to be his best man. At the rehearsal, two nights before the wedding, Jim blocked on almost every word he tried to say. I thought how important, and yet how emotional, the actual ceremony would be for him, and I wanted to do something that would give him the greatest possibility of being fluent as he said his marriage vows.

After lunch on the day of the wedding, Jim and I were left by ourselves with half an hour before we had to start for the church. We sat down together, and I told him I had in mind something that should help him through the ceremony. I slowed my own speech considerably but kept it flowing forward with the contacts loose, in a manner much like the one described in Dr. Van Riper's suggestion thirteen. I asked Jim to talk to me in the same way. He agreed, and he did it fluently enough. The time came to start for the church. On the way I kept him talking. We talked back and forth in this slow, loose way—which was really a form of fluent stuttering—about the traffic lights, about the kinds of trees we were passing, anything to keep him talking and to keep his mind from going into a rigid panic that would block his vows.

When we got to the church, the minister put us in an anteroom to wait for the organ signal. We kept right on talking, using that same speech. We didn't allow one moment of silence, and, as we talked, we focused on the feeling of our speech muscles moving.

Then came the organ signal, "Here Comes the Bride," and he went in. I stood arm against arm on Jim's right, his bride came up and stood close to him on his left, and he got through those vows without a hitch. I did sense at the very end that he was beginning to become tense, and, if he had had to say much more, he might have run into trouble, but as it was he was fine. Afterwards, in the receiving line, he stuttered, but it didn't matter a bit then. I don't take all the credit for that success—much goes to Dr. Van Riper, and much to Jim himself—but at least I had found a technique that worked for him.

■ ─── ■

Many stutterers are unrealistic people. They see their condition and prospects as being either much worse or much better than they actually are. I suppose it is human nature to avoid looking directly at a part of oneself that one wishes were not there; but I have been helped substantially by the practice of making determined, periodic efforts to recognize the extent of my current speech difficulties and, at the same time, to set up currently reasonable goals. The first time I did this deliberately was after my Chicago speech when I thought of giving slide shows. Even today, I know where the fences are on my own field—that is, how much I can expect to accomplish.

I have urged my cases to do the same thing. I have found that once a stutterer begins to take this kind of honest, practical attitude toward his situation his improvement is very likely to accelerate. Two persons upon whom I literally forced such confrontations were two young Australian men. Later, they became my lifelong friends. When I think of the way they felt about my early therapy, I can scarcely believe it.

Peter was an extremely severe stutterer who had gone through considerable therapy without any measurable improvement. When I first met him, I took him to dinner at the Hotel Australia in Sydney. After we had our menus and the waitress had asked for our orders, Peter indicated to me that he wanted tomato soup but that he was too blocked up to ask for it. I said to him, "You're going to ask the waitress for that, yourself. I'm not going to speak for you."

To the waitress I said, "Your job is to wait, and here's one time when that's just what you'll have to do." She smiled and said she didn't mind, while Peter, furious with me but trapped, tried to speak. When he was caught in a block, he would jerk his head violently in a manner that almost looked like epilepsy. It took him a long time, but he finally got the words out. I said, "Well, that's your first encounter with one of my ideas of effective therapy."

The other young man, John, was a violent stutterer who had been referred to me by Dr. Johnson. We met in Adelaide, in the airport, and I remember that on our way into town it took him several minutes to get out a single sentence. He was a person who I thought would benefit from some time at the Iowa speech clinic. I was able to persuade him and his family to make arrangements for him to go there.

The next year, when John arrived in the United States, I met him at the ship, we toured San Francisco, then I took him to the bus depot where he was going to catch a bus to Iowa City. We stood in line, getting nearer and nearer to the ticket window. John tried to put the money for his ticket into my hand, but I refused to take it. I said, "I won't do that for you."

When the clerk asked, "May I help you?," the poor fellow went into contortions. We held up that whole line. Everybody in it knew that I had the necessary information but that I was refusing to talk for John, and there was nearly a battle. After John finally blurted out that he wanted to go to Iowa City, I thought he might smash me in the face. I told him he'd just had a sample of American speech therapy and watched him, still fuming, climb onto his bus and be carried away.

I should add that the speech of both these men has improved tremendously. Peter is a married man with a family and a successful career. He still lives in Australia and is fluent enough, even on an overseas phone call. John became an American citizen and is now a psychology professor at one of our Southwest state universities, where his frequent lectures demonstrate adequate fluency.

In the fall of 1962 I went to the University of Denver to begin work on a Ph.D. in Speech Pathology. Much of the work I did there was under the able guidance of Dr. Ruth M. Clark, a professor who has a keen sense of the dynamics of the field and to whom I owe a debt of gratitude. My speech was generally good by then, although I still stuttered occasionally when I spoke up in classes. While I was studying at Denver, Sachiyuki Hamamoto came there from Japan to take courses that would permit him to receive a certificate in speech pathology from ASHA. We had many good times together.

At the end of my course work, I received a notice saying I had earned a 3.73 out of a possible 4.0 average. It made me wish there had been some way of telling the desperate freshman who nearly flunked out of Stanford with an 0.92 average that better days were coming.

When the time came to choose the subject for my dissertation, I ran into a snag. The professor who headed the deciding committee wanted me to do a psychological study, but, because I was already convinced that stuttering has an organic base, I wanted to take on a physiological project. The project that interested me most was concerned with masking noise.

I don't believe I asked Dr. Van Riper to intervene for me in this matter, but I did tell him about the problem. When he was in San Francisco for a speech conference in the autumn of 1964, he suggested that I bring the professor, whom he already knew, to his room in the San Francisco Hilton. There I watched the problem melt away. Dr. Van Riper told him that he thought I had a good idea: "I've been wallowing in this thing for fifty years and we haven't found the answer. It just could be that this is one little step that may help."

As soon as we were out in the hall, the professor said to me, "It sounds good. How soon can you send in your proposal?"

That was just one of several times that Dr. Van Riper has supported me when I needed him. He did it again shortly afterward when, in 1965, I was scheduled to appear on another panel at an ASHA national convention. The association was again meeting in Chicago, the scene of my 1956 catastrophe. In 1965 my fears were nowhere near what they had been on the earlier occasion—by this time I had myself pretty well in hand. But, naturally, I was nervous.

On the morning before the speech, I went out shopping with a friend. He seemed determined to go back to the hotel coffee shop for lunch, and, when we did, Dr. and Mrs. Van Riper came in and sat down at the table beside ours. We talked back and forth between the two tables. I felt the familiar steady kindness flowing from him; it was extremely welcome that day. The Van Ripers said they had to leave town right after lunch—later it occurred to me that Dr. Van Riper might have delayed their departure so that he could see me and give me a little encouragement. I asked my friend if he thought this too, and he did not deny it.

I don't remember blocking severely once in that speech. It was at times disrhythmic, but I thought I had improved on my 1956 performance about 97 percent.

■ ——————————————————————————————— ■

In the summer of 1965 I set up my masking noise experiment in New York City on the seventh floor of an old speech institute there. I had thirty stutterers run through tests in which, wearing headsets, they read aloud under five different masking noise conditions—no masking noise, random masking noise, noise controlled by the subjects, noise controlled by me, and solid masking noise. The passage that they read orally was three hundred words long, and it had been specially constructed so that all its sounds were in relative balance. The masking noise sounded like Niagara Falls.

Since a person cannot hear himself speaking when masking noise is operating, I hoped to find data significant for stutterers in the relationships between the noise, the hearing and proprioception feedback circuits, and the stutterers' speech. In the end I found that a slight majority of the stutterers consistently stopped stuttering under solid masking noise, but I had such mixed results that my chief contribution was probably that of ruling out possibilities.

I finished the work, wrote it up, and prepared for my Ph.D. oral exam. At first I thought I needed a unanimous vote from the examiners to pass, but after I learned, via a friendly secretary who tipped me off, that I only needed a simple majority, I felt more at ease about the "trial." Still, it was something to face. So when I read in one of Dr. West's studies that sugar can sometimes act as a spasm suppressant, I went out and bought a bag of the rock candy that looks like little squares of glass.

All that morning, while I looked over my dissertation, I kept a piece of the candy in my mouth, and when the time finally came for me to face the seven committee members, I went in and spoke the best under stress that I ever have in my life. I think the candy was mainly a placebo. The reason I did so well that day was more likely that I knew my material thoroughly—better than anyone else in the room.

When people who already hold the Ph.D. are talking to a candidate for the degree, they sometimes make me think of peacocks. Some of them wave their plumage around as if to show that they have the elegant feathers, but they aren't sure the candidate should have them too. At any rate, these "peacocks" were satisfied with my performance, and they decided to let me join them.

After I received my Ph.D., I accepted a position on the faculty at the University of New Hampshire, where I have taught ever since. I head the UNH stuttering program and am a member of the Department of Communication Disorders. I like my colleagues and my students at the university very much. The more I have lectured the easier it has become for me, and the more I have enjoyed it.

Durham, the home of the university, is in the southeastern part of the state, halfway between the White Mountains and Boston. It is easy to feel close to nature in this part of New England. I do a lot of walking near my home, and I like to watch the activity on the river that runs beside my house.

In warm weather I love to swim at a place called Wheelwright's Pond, not far away. Lake swimming has always appealed to me—I like the freshness of the water, the water lilies, and the rooty smells near the grassy shore. About five hundred feet out into Wheelwright's Pond there is a rock that rises nearly to the water's surface. The neighborhood children call it "Murray's Rock." It is a convenient spot for resting a bit and catching my breath when I take my usual swim across the lake and back. Every September when I feel the first chill in the water I wonder whether I'll be able to swim tomorrow. If it turns cold, then today's is the last swim of the year. There is a special feeling about that farewell. After it, I start looking forward to being back next year.

I can be in a hectic mood before going out to Wheelwright's; coming back I will be refreshed and recharged. Stutterers must make sure to include some kind of physical exercise in their regular routines. Reverting to the idea that structure precedes function, we must have bodies that are in good shape to perform at optimum levels. Rest is equally important. Being short of sleep always makes me more vulnerable to a tendency to stutter.

Along with physical exercise, mental tranquility is essential. Every stutterer needs either a quiet spot to which he can go or a place which he has managed to create within himself where he can be quiet and tune into his inner core. He must try to find an occupation that gives him satisfaction. And then, as I suggested to students in Chapter 7, he must reach out into the world in various ways to establish interests and relationships that enrich his life.

Much of my reaching out has combined the pleasures of nature and travel, such as a memorable trip to Norfolk, Virginia, in 1970 to see a total eclipse of the sun. Other enrichment has been intellectual, particularly my postdoctorate study at Harvard, an institution where my family ties date back to the 1690's. The interests which I enumerated in Chapter 9 have continued. Some of them, such as my fascination with Spain, have become interwoven with my professional life.

More than most people, stutterers must manage their lives in ways that will keep them below the threshold where significant stuttering starts to spill over. Ida Whitten, author of a 1938 *Quarterly Journal of Speech* article telling of her own victory over stuttering, still exemplifies, via fluency, this vital concept. It is important to keep oneself in good physical condition, to avoid fatigue and frequent overstimulation, and to stay away from unnecessary negative situations. Every stutterer should become sensitive to factors that seem consistently to result in increases or decreases in his stuttering. And then, having identified the positive elements, he must distribute them through his life in a way that will bring him as close as possible to homeostasis, the state of harmonious balance.

The author with Marie-Claude Lalique in front of Lasserre Restaurant in Paris, April, 1980. Left to right: Madame Boulenger, Madame Lalique, and the author.

It may be noted that this memorable event at Lasserre, together with other factors, served as a motivator to undertake studies in French, starting from "ground zero" at age 54. An intensive, demanding course at the renowned Institut de Français at Villefranche-Sur-Mer on the French Riviera paid off handsomely. It is now possible to converse adequately in French, even to lecture in it, given sufficient preparation. This accomplishment has been deeply rewarding in all aspects.

23

Questions and Answers

In my teaching and lecturing, I am often asked a number of questions about stuttering. Therefore, in this final chapter, I have included some of these questions and the answers I give to them.

What happens to a person's stuttering as he gets older?

Whether or not a person undergoes therapy, his stuttering will probably diminish markedly as the years go by. W. Somerset Maugham was apparently an exception to this rule—his stuttering persisted noticeably into his old age. I have known only one stutterer with such a history. He was a minister who went on delivering weekly sermons until he died. More significant, probably, than the sermon pressure is that this man's personal life was always full of strain.

Psychological explanations for the usual decrease in stuttering begin with the distinct role changes that most people experience as they grow older. Most of them have given up trying to do things they can't do well, and, instead, have developed their strengths. Often they are respected for what they have accomplished, and they have a gratifying feeling of being established in their career areas and in their communities. A pleasant sense of confidence and authority comes with experience. Most older people care less about others' opinions—the searching for status that teenagers go through is behind them. Philosophically, most older adults don't get as emotionally upset about minor problems as younger ones do. They also have learned that "compromise" is not a bad word.

And, older people slow down physically. I love Dr. Van Riper's story from his young adult days about an old farmer he once met in a corn field. Dr. Van Riper said he could tell by the fluent enough but rather choppy way the farmer was speaking that he must have once stuttered badly. Dr. Van Riper asked the man if he had ever been a stutterer. "Oh yes," he said. "I used to be a terrible stutterer, used to jump around and spit and sputter worse than you do, but I'm too old and too tired to do that now."

■ ─── ■

What do stutterers mean when they use the word "guilt" in describing their feelings? Guilty of what?

Stuttering has been one of our society's most penalized handicaps. Most stutterers learn very early in their lives that it is desirable not to stutter. Society rewards them for fluency, and the implication is clear that when they do not speak fluently they are doing something wrong. When we do something wrong, we feel guilty about it.

Stutterers often feel guilty about making their listeners wait for replies, or about unattractive sounds and facial contortions that may repel their listeners, or at least make their listeners feel uncomfortable.

In Chapter 1, I described my guilt when as a small child I saw that my stuttering was making my mother suffer socially.

When a stutterer begins to practice avoidance maneuvers, he feels guilty about pretending to be a person different from the person he really is.

In novels, bad characters used to "stutter guiltily" when they were confronted with the proof of their crimes. The association between stuttering and actual guilt is an ancient one; thus, in therapy a stutterer has to work consciously to sever that mental relationship. As Dr. Sheehan has said, one must learn that it is possible to stutter without feeling guilty about it and that it is possible to feel guilty about something without going into a stuttering block.

■ ─── ■

How useful is bouncing as a therapy technique today?

Unlike the slide or the prolongation, which many present-day therapists teach stutterers so that they can go ahead and speak in a more streamlined form of stuttering, bouncing is used infrequently. I believe that Dr. Sheehan, who originally taught me the bounce, does not recommend it at all now, except possibly as a technique for stutterers to use when they demonstrate to the outside world that they stutter.

I occasionally see individuals whose stuttering is so extreme that their speech mechanism seems to have entirely lost its coordination. This kind of stuttering makes me think of a freight train that is swaying out of control, on the verge of leaving the track. Bouncing sometimes can be used effectively with stuttering such as this, to help the stutterer rechannel his speech energy flow.

Then there is the case of the internalized stutterer who signs up for therapy, even though he may speak more fluently than his therapist, even though—in rare cases—he may not remember ever really stuttering at all. He may come in and say, "I think that I'm going to stutter," or, "I'm in a state of terrible anxiety because I think my speech may fall apart."

It may turn out that long ago the patient stuttered a little, and, perhaps because of his family's alarmed reaction to that stuttering, he has repressed all memory of the experience and has been unable to repress the fear that he may stutter again. Other internalized stutterers may have a physical or a psychological tendency toward stuttering which they sense, even though it has never been realized. A still different form of internalized stuttering is that in which the person never stutters audibly—in his speech there are spaces in which he seems to be doing nothing; in actuality, he is stuttering silently.

In order to treat these people, the therapist or the pathologist should get them to bring up some stuttering. Usually, because they are fighting inwardly to hide the handicap, they are terrified at the idea of making a stuttering sound. Sometimes the therapist can produce stuttering by putting a person in a conflict situation and telling him not to use any resistance at all, to let what is going to happen occur naturally. If the stuttering will not surface under those conditions, bouncing, along with other techniques that simulate stuttering, can be used to make it appear.

Internalized stutterers are rather rare. Some of them need psychiatric as well as speech therapy. Stutterers with symptoms that show may be luckier because they have something to begin to work on right away.

■ ──────────────────────────────────── ■

Why do you believe that stuttering has an organic basis?

We have accumulated evidence that there are slight but definite physical differences between stutterers as a group and normal speakers. Biochemists have established differences in blood patterns between stutterers and nonstutterers. A difference in the nervous system's operation is indicated by the discovery that during stuttering spasms the pupils in the eyes of stutterers do not contract the way normal speakers' pupils do.

In Chapter 2, I described briefly the cerebral dominance theory of stuttering which states that stuttering may result from a brief stoppage in the nervous system, involving the timed nerve impulses that are sent from the two halves of the brain down to the speech muscles on the two sides of the jaw. This stoppage may occur because neither of the brain hemispheres is clearly in control of speech; the two may actually be competing for control. If both sets of muscles do not receive the impulses at the same split second, a tiny break in speech results. In an article on stuttering which he wrote for *The Atlantic Monthly* in 1939, Dr. Van Riper has recalled a 1930's experiment in which he took part:

> . . . In one of the most crucial of the subsequent experiments, needle electrodes were inserted into the paired jaw muscles of a stutterer, one on each side of his face. While he talked freely or stuttered, the little electrical currents accompanying the nervous impulses to these muscles were amplified and photographed. As one of the guinea pigs in this experiment, I recall not only the needles but also the atmosphere of delighted discovery that filled the laboratory when it was found that during my occasional spells of normal speech the nervous impulses arrived regularly in both the right and left jaw muscles, whereas they came down to only one of those muscles when I stuttered. Other stutterers showed the same results. Normal speakers had perfectly synchronized nervous impulses even when they pretended to stutter very badly.

In his book, *The Nature of Stuttering,* Dr. Van Riper describes a 1966 operation performed by a surgeon named R. K. Jones which supports the cerebral dominance theory:

> Jones, a neurosurgeon, was preparing to operate on four patients who had stuttered severely since childhood but who had recently developed brain pathology, and he had decided to use a new technique pioneered by Wada (1949). The technique consisted of injecting sodium amytol directly into first the right and then the left carotid arteries while the patient is conscious and talking. As Wada and Rasmussen (1960) demonstrated, when this drug is introduced into the system in this way, a temporary aphasia results, provided the artery serving the dominant hemisphere of the brain is the one injected. To his surprise, Jones found that all four of these stutterers developed transient aphasia when the drug was injected into *either* the right or left carotid arteries, thus indicating that they had a bilateral cortical control of speech, that there were "speech centers" in both hemispheres. Jones then performed his surgery on the damaged hemisphere and found that complete remission of stuttering took place in all his patients. After recovery, he administered the sodium amytol as before and discovered that now the exstutterers became aphasic only when one artery was injected (the one serving the nonoperated hemisphere). They no longer had cortical representation for speech in both hemispheres but only in one. Jones remarks that "the results on stammering of a one-sided operation for unrelated lesions in these four patients were quite startling and can only be explained by the view that stammering is associated with an interference by one hemisphere with the speech performance of the other."

In 1975 I received a letter from Dr. Travis, who was an important pioneer in applying the cerebral dominance theory to stuttering, but who later (when I knew him at USC) became enthusiastic about psychoanalytic explanations for the perpetuation of stuttering. In the letter, Dr. Travis said that his newest research had convinced him that stuttering does have an organic base. He described new brain wave studies showing that in stutterers, speech-related activities were substantially represented on both sides of the brain, while the brain waves of normal speakers indicated a decided preference for one side only.

These studies and others like them convince me that while mixed dominance may not be the whole answer to the question of what causes stuttering it must certainly somehow often figure in that answer.

Today a number of researchers are concerned with the possibility that stuttering might be physically linked to the central hearing process. In their work, these researchers employ a technique called Delayed Auditory Feedback, "DAF" for short, in which stutterers wearing headphones hear the words they have just spoken a fraction of a second after they would normally hear them. Anyone who has given a speech under circumstances where a microphone and loudspeakers produce this effect knows how distracting it can be. Stutterers who have been working to increase their physical awareness of their own speech mechanism movements use the DAF machine to create a situation in which they can speak evenly only if they are able to resist what they hear. They must pay no attention to the machine's distracting sounds; instead, they must concentrate on the movements of their lips, tongue, and jaw (proprioceptive movements), depending on these to steer their mechanisms smoothly through word sequences.

Studies of heredity are important when one is trying to determine if stuttering has an organic basis, because characteristics that repeat in families frequently reflect the members' genetic or physical makeups. In Chapter 2, I mentioned a study by Dr. Bryngelson that found stutterers to have relatives with the handicap eight times more often than normal speakers do. The latest figures I have from the other genetic study I mentioned in that chapter, one going on at Yale University, show that more than twenty percent of the stutterers in that program were found to have fathers who stutter, and more than six percent of them have mothers who stutter. The percentages for normal speakers are far below these.

There are other genetic findings that show stutterers to have unusually high percentages of characteristics in common. Stuttering occurs unusually often in families that include multiple births, such as twins or triplets. There are unusually high percentages of stutterers who are left-handed—a fact that may relate back to the cerebral dominance theory. I have already stated that there are four or five times more male stutterers than female. Some authorities believe that this significant difference reflects the more demanding character of male roles in society. Others believe that, on the whole, males are organically weaker than females. They point for further proof to the larger incidences of epilepsy, color blindness, and deaths at birth among boys, compared to girls. The statistics indicate that genetic factors may have precipitated the disorder in the cases of many stutterers, but probably not in all.

Opponents of the organic theory, such as Dr. Johnson, have said that stutterers are more likely to develop in families with a history of stuttering because those families are unusually sensitive to the appearance of stuttering-like symptoms. As I have already written, members of these families are apt to pounce on the symptoms, label them "stuttering," and by making the child nervous and self-conscious about his speech, actually encourage his becoming a stutterer.

A number of studies have been made to test this explanation for the high incidence of stutterers in families with a stuttering history. One of the most interesting investigated the histories of children who were born into families where stuttering had existed, but who at birth had been taken out of that environment and reared in homes where stuttering was unknown. Although these children had no direct contact with their original families, there was a much higher incidence of stuttering among them than there was in a comparison group of adopted children who had no stuttering family histories.

In February, 1977, Dr. Sheehan and his daughter, Marian Sheehan Costley, published an article in the *Journal of Speech and Hearing Disorders* called "A Reexamination of the Role of Heredity in Stuttering." In a section entitled "Contact with the Stutterer," they refer to a study in which, of thirty stutterers who knew that there was stuttering in their families, thirteen had no direct contact with the other family stutterers— "impressive evidence in favor of some kind of genetic factor in stuttering. Johnson's contention that stuttering runs in families primarily on a cultural basis appears to be contradicted. . . ."

Convincing as they are, none of these reports and studies persuades me that stuttering has a physical basis more strongly than does the comparison of the speech of stutterers with that of normal speakers: There are differences in the *kind* of speaking that I hear in each group. Examples of this difference may be found in the Chapter 2 comparisons between the so-called stuttering that is common in the speech of normal children and the stuttering speech of young stutterers.

The difference appears to exist between the speech of stutterers and normal speakers of all ages, not just the speech of children. Stuttering is essentially a timing disorder. There are breaks in the tempo or flow of even a stutterer's fluent speech that are, in most cases, different from the normal speaker's breaks. The stutterer's breaks are involuntary. It is as though there are occasional, brief short circuits, resulting in a mild disrhythm—tiny pauses before some words and slight extra pressure on some syllables.

These minute irregularities are what I think of as organic stuttering residuals, which one may never get rid of, but which can be handled in ways that make them hardly noticeable. What most stutterers have done is to superimpose a handicap made up of complicated psychological reactions and learned maneuvers upon this organic deficit.

Fortunately, these psychological malreactions can be largely undone, even though the undoing almost always requires sustained hard work. I believe that I have my own stuttering basically reduced to the bare residual level now.

Dr. West aptly stated what summarizes most of the foregoing when, in a speech given in 1960, he said, "Stuttering is caused by a weakness affecting the speech mechanism. Stuttering is perpetuated by a continuation of that weakness, or by a morbid awareness of it, or by a combination of these two factors."

To understand better the scope of this weakness, we need a more far-reaching, clearer perspective of the anomaly of stuttering. This would be analogous to viewing the sea from an airplane far above it. We could spot some of the questionable areas and get a better idea of their extent. At present, our limited view of stuttering is similar to that of viewing the sea from the beach. It is hard to depict the degree, form, and direction of formations lying beneath the surface and of the currents as well.

▪ ————————————————————————————— ▪

What further challenges does a stutterer meet, once he begins to improve?

Stuttering's high visibility and its unusually frustrating nature are strong motivators which push many stutterers to keep trying to improve. It may be harder to find the necessary incentive to conquer a handicap that can be hidden. But, because speech improvement is a long and inconsistent business, full of unpleasant requirements that the individual cannot evade, the improving stutterer should consistently look for additional sources of motivation that will help him through the work's discouraging periods.

Strong motivation is also necessary because much of the work is done on one's own. The stutterer has to put himself through solitary learning experiences, one after the other, since the therapist often can do no more than direct from a distance. After I made Peter order his own tomato soup, he had to go on in his life to other restaurants by himself. After John, standing beside me, managed to say "Iowa City" to the man selling bus tickets, he had to find out by himself how to get to the university campus, and then to the clinic, and on to countless other destinations beyond that. As Dr. Sheehan once said, "You have to stutter your own way out of it."

■ ———————————————————————————————— ■

The severe stutterer thinks of words as objects to be dealt with in sequence. He copes with each moment as it occurs, going from one trauma to the next. It's a little like driving a car on a rocky road and focusing on each rock that the car goes over.

Dr. Bluemel has written about the improving stutterer's need to reorganize speech, and about the way this involves reorganizing his thinking. Stutterers are often so distracted by their handicap that they think as well as speak in fits and starts. As both control and automaticity increase, the stutterer must learn to think in larger groupings, to experience single thoughts that are made of groups of words, first in phrases and clauses, then in whole sentences, and, finally to think, as Dr. Van Riper once put it, of "paragraphs followed by 'Very Truly Yours.'" Our driver is learning to stop focusing three or four feet beyond his car's hood to see what he is going to hit next; he is lifting his gaze to look a block ahead. And then, on open highways when he feels easy and free, he will begin to look miles ahead, sometimes all the way to the horizon.

When he is constantly monitoring his speech, still going from word to word, still continually exercising control, the stutterer will usually speak in a monotone. As he relaxes and begins to think in larger units, his speech will begin to vary in its tone in a normal speaker's way, the variations reflecting the speaker's desire to give different emphasis to different groups of words. A parenthetical phrase which follows and describes a noun might naturally be delivered in a lower, softer tone than that used for the noun, which would naturally be emphasized.

At the time that these adjustments are taking place, most stutterers find that they must also cope with the problem of disrhythms. The whittling down of severe blockages often leaves gaps even in a person's relaxed speech, gaps into which stuttering can easily flow again, and which must be closed.

I found that I could make headway in this area by doing some simple exercises. One was to take a stopwatch and keep track of the speed with which I could read orally, working by sentence and by paragraph. I might take a sentence which a normal speaker could deliver in thirteen seconds, but which was taking me twenty-two, and make a commitment to get it out in seventeen. Then I'd work till I achieved that time, all the while trying to maintain smooth fluency. This exercise is a hard one, but it forces the speaker in beneficial ways.

Another, easier, exercise is that of shadowing a television or a radio speaker, repeating his words a second or two after he says them, trying to maintain his pace and to imitate his tone. This helps to increase one's speed and to promote word grouping without gaps, and with normal tone variation as well.

At the time when I was doing these exercises most diligently I had not heard of the work of Dr. Eugene McDonald, a Pennsylvania State University authority in the field of articulation. Paralleling Dr. Bluemel's thought reorganization ideas, Dr. McDonald concentrated on sound alone in speech grouping. He wrote that we do not speak word by word, but in groups of syllables that usually contain a number of words. He described ballistic movements in normal speech, the shooting out of whole thought groupings in a flow of rapid fire syllables. It is this ballistic action that the stutterer must eventually master when his speech is free.

But, of course, it will not always be completely free. In the middle of fluent, automatic speech there will be times when the stutterer all at once finds himself in trouble. Fear or pressure of some kind is present, and then the only thing for him to do is to slow down and to consciously take control, deliberately guiding the mechanism through the block, keeping the flow, keeping a difficult word from fragmenting.

When this happens to me, I sometimes feel as though I am suddenly operating with molasses in my system. My voice drops. My words per minute rate is probably cut in half. I am tending to my speech, fitting in some of the old patterns, allowing some malformation in my mouth and some stuttering if necessary, but pulling out of it very easily, integrating until I feel free emotionally again, until I can look a hundred miles ahead in the desert and can return to speaking quickly without thinking about it.

As an improved stutterer begins to move back and forth between automaticity and control, his speech will suffer from abrupt rate changes. He can learn to soften the edges between these states to make them less apparent to his listeners. To return once more to our driver analogy, anybody who has learned to drive a shift car knows about the gradual increase in shifting skill that comes with practice. As both the driver and the stutterer respond to the needs of the moment, they can learn in time to make smooth transitions in the focus of their attentions and in the physical adjustment of their machines.

■ ————————————————————————————— ■

What would you say to a stutterer who wants to go into therapy and who asks you for advice?

First of all, he should look around and find out all he can about the therapies that are available and then try to talk to people who have been through each one. Many different kinds of stuttering therapy have been developed, and all of them have had some degree of success with some stutterers. Even the much-maligned commercial stuttering schools which flourished in the United States in the early part of this century helped some people. The late Dr. John Fletcher of Tulane University said that it is too bad stuttering yields to so many different kinds of treatment, because if it didn't, we would have more ideas about its cause.

One of the many maddening things about the treatment of stuttering is that a therapy which works for one person may not work for another. Probably the most famous example of this occurred in the early 1930's, shortly after Charles Van Riper went to The University of Iowa speech clinic for help with his stuttering. Part of the time he acted as a chauffeur for Dr. Travis, and his stuttering was so severe that when he drove up to filling stations he could hardly ask for gas.

He spent several months in therapy, often under Dr. Bryngelson, who had him work through voluntary stuttering to gain control over his involuntary blocks. During those months he made remarkable improvement. Within a year he had learned to talk well enough so that he could start to teach.

Dr. Johnson was at Iowa then. He had made some headway with his stuttering by this time, but it was still a serious problem for him. He saw Charles Van Riper's stuttering fading away, and he was so impressed that he put himself on a similar program. Immediately, his stuttering became so much worse that he was told to stop speaking altogether and to go off on a week-long fishing trip, during which he was to continue his silence.

There is no easy answer to the question of why a therapy will work with one person and not with another. Part of the answer must have to do with the personality of the stutterer. For example, for some people, the kind of therapy in which they are repeatedly forced to confront their own avoiding behavior is so unpleasant that it will probably not work for them. Such people might be more successful in a program that concentrates on work with the symptom itself. Many stutterers have tried various remedies on their own before seeking a therapist. These people may already have a fair idea of the approaches that will help them, and the kinds that won't. If, once a therapy has been given a fair trial, the stutterer feels that the direction of the work goes with his psychological grain the therapy is likely to move ahead in a profitable way.

Research has shown that a vital key to the success of a therapy is the quality of the relationship between the stutterer and his therapist. If the stutterer feels that the therapist is genuinely interested in his case, that the therapist cares about him and wants to share some of his experience, no matter what kind of therapy is being practiced, it is bound to meet with some success. Stutterers need especially to feel that they are not alone with their problem. If a stutterer has confidence in the person helping him, he will relax and set aside much of his fear, establishing conditions that are always beneficial to stuttering improvement.

The late John Clancy, a former director of the Shady Trails Speech Improvement Camp in Michigan, saw over the years many groups of stutterers working under clinicians who subscribed to very different theories about stuttering. He said he defied anyone to prove that one therapy was better than another. He said the major factor in a therapy's success was whether the clinician administering it could develop enthusiasm and acceptance in the spirits of the youngsters in his charge.

Regardless of the therapy, another, and crucial, determiner of a therapy's success is what I call the stutterer's ripeness, or his readiness to change. Many stutterers who say they want to get better are actually deeply resistant to the exposure that stuttering therapy entails, to the threat of having to confront a part of themselves that they've tried for many years to sweep out of consciousness, or possibly to the loss of a crutch that has kept them from having to accept the responsibilities of normal life.

There are many qualities that go into the condition of ripeness. Among them are flexibility, determination, patience, discipline, and self-understanding. These attributes are mainly attitudinal ones. The stutterer's attitude, as research conducted by Dr. Barry Guitar of The University of Vermont has revealed, is often a significant factor in the outcome of therapy.

■ ─── ■

Therapies that focus on behavior modification are concerned with physical behavior. They make very little attempt to work with the patient's emotions. Clinicians working with these therapies say that once the symptom is relieved, the feelings will take care of themselves.

Although I question this, I do not intend to ignore the value of systems that can be learned quickly and that can give a stutterer little or no abnormality in speaking. The major question I must ask is how well will the techniques stand up over a long period of time, as the people using them embark into the world with its surprises and strains—how automatic can these techniques become so that the individuals do not have to work continually at doing something intended to prevent them from stuttering. The automaticity of speech, like the automaticity of breathing, will eventually seek expression and break through any consciously controlled, continually monitored speech. One is incapable of maintaining an automatic act at a volitionally directed level at all times.

The wide acceptance of intensive, short-term therapies that often incorporate behavior modification techniques is relatively new. We have not yet received enough data about their long-range effectiveness.

In regard to the intensity of these therapies, I think intense, full-time therapy for several weeks is better than therapy for an hour once or twice a week for a year. One drawback to most of these types of programs, however, is that their formal therapy ends too abruptly. There is not enough follow-up or maintenance therapy to support the people after they leave the therapy centers. More regular, preferably direct, contact with clinicians trained in the therapy should go on after the basic program, and it should continue for at least a year.

I also think that behavior modification programs should provide for exchanges between the stutterers, who, working under terrific pressure, can meet to vent some of their feelings. Most of these programs allow for no specific time for such exchanges—I suppose if the participants are not too worn out, they may share their reactions to the experience before and after the programs each day.

Dr. Sheehan has said that a person's stuttering problem is like an iceberg. The part that shows, that can be seen and heard, is very small. Underneath, unseen, is the rest of the problem—vast, complex, made up of the person's memories, his avoidance maneuvers, his anxieties and his expectations, and so on. I used to think that therapy to be effective must be addressed to all the interacting parts of the problem, not just to the symptomatic part that shows.

However, I am now inclined to encourage stutterers who want to try the short-cut, symptom-controlling techniques that have been developed in qualified programs, especially if they can work out a satisfactory follow-up system that will actively support them afterwards for a year. For some people it may be best to work first on pure behavior, to find out what aspects of their larger problem disappear as the symptom comes under control, and then to attend to whatever difficulties remain.

■ ── ■

While I know that every therapy has something to recommend it, there are four cautions that I offer to anyone who asks me for advice about choosing a therapy:

1. Whatever therapy a stutterer adopts, it should be one that results in his speaking with a relatively normal speech pattern flow. This is why the technique of stuttering fluently has such enormous appeal for me. A person who can speak in an apparently normal way is going to be miles ahead of one who, even though his stuttering is not very apparent, is left with a speech flow pattern that is distinctly abnormal. The stutterer must eventually get to the point where most of his speech is automatic, spoken without self-conscious thought.

In the beginning of therapy, when the very severe stutterer is learning to handle blockages, he will probably have to go through a period in which he is almost always doing certain things to guard his speech. But excessive monitoring is distracting and exhausting and is virtually impossible to maintain constantly. It makes me think of the centipede who was happy—

> . . . until the frog in fun
> Said, "Pray, which leg comes after which?"
> This raised his mind to such a pitch,
> He lay distracted in the ditch,
> Considering how to run.

Eventually the improving stutterer must reach a point where most of the time his speech flows automatically, and he can focus his attention on what he wants to say.

2. While it is important for a stutterer to keep working at reducing his symptoms, the better therapies are the ones that do not put a premium on complete suppression of stuttering. The stutterer should always leave room for natural disfluency, and, occasionally, some possible stuttering—to try to cut these off forever is both unrealistic and dangerous.

3. The stutterer should be wary of a therapy that leaves him speaking fluently, but still maneuvering to avoid feared words or speaking situations that he is afraid will make him stutter. For such fluency a high price in psychic energy is paid.

4. The stutterer should aim for a state in which he can speak with a minimal amount of effort and control—where the speech is as good as it can be without his having to sacrifice too much emotional freedom. This might be called the optimum level of performance. Each individual has to find his own. As he does, he will lose most of his fear of speaking. He will develop a capacity to go ahead and a willingness to be himself, without pretense. He will become master of his speech, and not its slave.

■ ——————————————————————————————————— ■

A stutterer who achieves real improvement learns more than speech management. As for myself, I learned to be realistic, to keep trying in spite of discouragement, and to take care of myself. My journey from the state of severe stutterer to that of sufficiently fluent speaker was hardly a trip that I would ever have chosen to undertake, but it was fated for me, and, in many ways, the experience has been a fascinating and a valuable one.

*Major Self-Help Groups
for Stutterers in the U.S.A.*

National Stuttering Project
2151 Irving Street
San Francisco, CA 94122-1609

Speak Easy International
233 Concord Drive
Paramus, NJ 07652

National Council on Stuttering
558 Russell Road
DeKalb, IL 60115

STUTTERING
FOUNDATION
OF AMERICA

FORMERLY SPEECH FOUNDATION OF AMERICA
*A Non-Profit Organization
Since 1947 —
Helping Those Who Stutter*

P.O. Box 11749 • Memphis, TN 38111-0749